My Journey to Betterment

Brigadier General George M. Shuffer, Jr., United States Army, Retired.

My Journey to Betterment

An Autobiography

George Macon Shuffer, Junior
Brigadier General, US Army
Retired

VANTAGE PRESS
New York

SECOND EDITION

Copyright © 2003 by George Macon Shuffer, Junior

Published by Vantage Press, Inc.
516 West 34th Street, New York, New York 10001

Manufactured in the United States of America
ISBN: 0-533-12654-1

Library of Congress Catalog Card No.: 97-91373

0 9 8 7 6 5 4 3 2 1

To my wife Cecilia and our children, who sacrificed much to help unfold the story

Contents

Preface

Born the great-grandson of white slave owners and black slaves in Palestine, Texas, in 1923, I sensed early on that my social setting was the main obstacle to betterment. Stifling Jim Crow laws, race hatred, poverty, and apathy made upward mobility difficult for whites and highly improbable for blacks. I prayed for the intelligence and strength to overcome the obstructions and rise above the milieu.

I studied intensely in school to make all A's and longed to graduate from college with honors. Even in extracurricular activities, which came hard for me, I strove to be the best. When converted to the Church, I wanted to do more than passively believe.

My parents were too poor to send me to college, and I could not find meaningful employment in the civilian world; so I joined the army, hoping for a better life.

Serving thirty-five years, I fought in World War II, Korea, and Vietnam as a combat infantry officer (winning gallantry and valorous duty medals in all three), married, fathered and raised eleven children (all singles of the same mother), earned a masters degree in History from the University of Maryland, graduated from the U.S. Army War College, and rose in rank from private to brigadier general. After army retirement, I gained ordination to the Holy Order of Deacon in the Roman Catholic Church.

I attribute my life and achievements to the grace of God, remembering that: *With the Lord, you can do all things; without Him, you can do nothing* (John 15:5).

My Journey to Betterment

1
Roots

The earliest I can trace my family roots is to 1812. That year Johann (John) M. Sheffer, my great-grandfather, came to birth in Ohio of Germanic immigrants. John, the youngest of four boys, grew up on his father's small farm near Marietta, learning expert agricultural skills. He dreamed of making his fortune with land and slaves growing cotton in the South, for there was an insatiable demand for this commodity the world over.

Floating down the Ohio and Mississippi Rivers in 1833 to the ten-thousand acre Olivier Plantation in Louisiana, he took on the job of junior overseer. He believed he could get more effort and work product out of slaves that he supervised by being firm but kind and gentle. He often worked in the steamy sun alongside them, and he insisted on letting them rest on Sundays. He taught them skills that he learned from his father and tended the sick among them. His slaves came to respect and love him so much that they worked extra hard to double, even triple, production over previous years. In the course of eight years, he got promoted from junior to master overseer, gaining Olivier's ardent respect and confidence.

Olivier and John agreed that John would take ownership, for a modest sum, of a thousand-acre tract in west-central Louisiana near Shreveport. John would share ten percent of his cotton profits with Olivier for shipping his crops through Olivier's Red River front wharf in Shreveport.

John acquired ten slaves in 1844 and began plantation production of cotton on his own land. Among the slaves he bought was Catherine Clay, a light-skinned mulatto, who was born in Virginia in 1822 and sold south to Louisiana in 1844. John had sexual intercourse with Catherine; she conceived, and she gave birth to Jacob John Sheffer, my grandfather, in 1849.

Slave Jacob grew up on his father's plantation benign to slave life, because John treated him like a legitimate son. Jacob did not relish bondage, but he used its environment and his father's kind teaching to learn proficient agrarian techniques and develop the knack for animal husbandry. He had a premonition one day that he would own a farm and demonstrate his equality with whites.

After Emancipation, Jacob remained with his father, working for pay through 1869. Early the next year, he got a stake from John and went to Vistula, Texas, an unincorporated settlement of 190 souls (mostly black), in Houston County. He purchased some livestock and 150 acres of cheap but fertile land. Before the purchase he changed his surname to *Shuffer,* most probably to conceal his slave background. (Slaves normally took the surname of their master.) The concealment attempt failed, because word of his former bondage got to Vistula not long after he arrived. He kept the changed name anyway.

Afterward, he expanded his land holding to 500 acres by buying smaller black-owned farms and grazing areas contiguous with his. As his herds multiplied and his crops flourished, he became one of the leading farmers in southwest Houston County and the envy of many regional whites.

Unlike his soft-spoken, mild-mannered father, Jacob was stern and domineering, especially with blacks in his hire. He readily inflicted whip lashes on slackers with threats to cut their pay. Blacks throughout the community looked up to him more out of fear than genuine respect. At the same time, he was contentious with whites, refusing to play the typically docile, subservient black. He never removed his hat or bowed to them, nor addressed them as "sir" or "ma'am."

In 1875 Jacob married Fannie Munn, a former slave girl, who experienced nativity in Georgia, February 1857. She migrated to Vistula in 1874 when the community's population began to rise. Fannie's parents are unknown, although she claimed to be of Cherokee Indian and black heritage. Jacob and Fannie had four sons and six daughters, all in Vistula. George Macon

2

Fannie Munn, circa 1928.

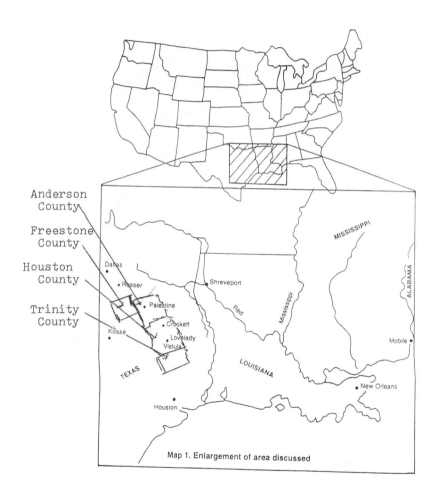

Anderson
County

Freestone
County

Houston
County

Trinity
County

Dallas
Rosser
Palestine
Crockett
Kosse
Lovelady
Vistula
TEXAS

Shreveport
Red
MISSISSIPPI
Mississippi
LOUISIANA
New Orleans
Houston
ALABAMA
Mobile

Map 1. Enlargement of area discussed

"GM" Shuffer, Sr., my father, was their number-five child. He was born on September 4, 1883. Their other children in order of birth were: Pearley (female) born 1876, Caswell (female) born 1878, Lona (female) born 1880, Garfield (male) born July 1881, Elizabeth (female) born September 1885, Hanneth (female) born July 7, 1887, Waymon (male) born November 1890, Laujanice (female) born January 1893, and Survine (male) born August 25, 1895.

My mother, Johnnie D'Ella Butler, has a known family line reaching back to circa 1840. In that time, Alabama-born Captain William Butler, my great-grandfather on Johnnie's side, bought slaves to grow cotton on a rented portion of an unknown owner's plantation. Martha Lacy, one of his slaves, born in 1835, gave birth by him to William "Will" Butler, my grandfather, in 1857.

As the Civil War drew to its close, Captain Butler, seeking more peaceful surroundings, took his slaves by coastal and river craft from Mobile to Shreveport, then west overland to Rosser, Texas, and established a farm. On a farm nearby, slave owner Ian Woodruff had fathered two slave girls by his housekeeper and cook, Mary Vinson. They were: Ida Mae, born on September 18, 1863, and Ellen, born in May 1865. Ida was my grandmother.

Young slave Will Butler persuaded his master, Captain Butler, to buy Ida, whom he admired, from her master, Woodruff. He did, and he allowed Will and Ida to grow up together on his farm after slaves were freed in Texas on June 19, 1865. Captain Butler believed that enslaving blacks was a benevolent act of charity to God's most neglected brethren. Paternal control of the life and care of Negroes to him meant not only reaping material benefits from their labors here on earth, but also that through his loving care of them, he was working out his salvation in heaven.

In 1880, Will, then in his early twenties and with a stake from his generous father, took Ida to Kosse, Texas, and married her. Afterward, they moved to Vistula, bought 240 acres of land, and spent their life careers farming and ranching. They had eleven children. Their number-five child was Johnnie, born August 31, 1888. Their other children in order of birth were: Forrest (male) born in 1880, Florida (female) born in 1882, George (male) born in 1884, Willie (male) born in 1886, Luther (male) born in

5

Will and Ida Butler, with children Augusta, Maud, and Luther, c. 1895.

1889, Augusta (female) born in 1891, Maud (female) born in 1893, Noble (male) born in 1895, Jay (male) born in 1898, and Fay (male) born in 1900.

By 1900 Jacob's farm had reached its full potential. All but his two younger children, ages four and six, were able to help work his expanded acreage to supply several farmers' markets in the region. Yet, to optimize profits from his livestock, cotton, and corn crops, he needed the assistance of five hired hands, all black.

One of his recently employed was Custer Harris, an ex-convict with an assumed name, who was unaware of Jacob's temper and aversion to lazy louts, especially those with hangovers from drunkenness the night before. Custer showed up drunk and late for work one day in March 1901. He promptly received ten whip lashes and a warning to expect worse if he ever got drunk again. Angry and afraid of Jacob, Custer harbored a deep grudge and growing hatred of him, vowing to get revenge.

Early one Sunday morning in June, he seized the opportunity. Jacob customarily inspected his crops and fence line on horseback every Sunday morning before worship service, invariably following pronounced fence line trails. Custer, in ambush from a brush area close to the fence trail, shot and killed Jacob with a 12-gauge shotgun, hitting him in the head and back as he rode by. Custer fled the area, but he was caught the next day by Sheriff John Bruton near the Trinity County line. He was convicted for the assassination and sentenced to Huntsville penitentiary for twenty years. He got paroled after serving only two years, but he never returned to Houston County. White enemies of the Shuffers, especially the local Ku Klux Klan, were pleased by Jacob's demise. They longed to see the day when all those uppity Shuffers would vanish from the county.

Fannie bitterly grieved Jacob's death. She was intelligent and quick of wit, but illiterate, with little capacity to manage or lead. Three of Jacob's six daughters survived him. They were Pearley, who had married and left the farm; Elizabeth, who died of pneumonia two years after Jacob died; and Hanneth, who married and left home shortly after his murder. This left his four sons at the farm: Garfield (almost 21), GM (18), Waymon (10),

Jacob J. Shuffer's tombstone, Black Vistula Cemetery.

and Survive (5). As between Garfield and GM, the latter possessed better ability to manage, so Fannie put him in charge. Garfield thought surely he would be given the reins. Jealous and sadly disappointed, he grudgingly remained at home, but he openly sought to leave as soon as something better came along.

GM graduated from the county school system the same month that Jacob died. He wanted to enter Prairie View Normal College for Negroes in Texas the following September, but he decided to remain in active charge of the farm until Garfield could learn management techniques well enough to keep production thriving.

Lean, strong, and handsome, with a shrewd mind, GM copied many traits and attributes of his father. Standing exactly six feet tall at age eighteen, he not only won the admiration of his mother, but also the respect of Garfield and the hired hands.

One day he noticed Ruth Smith, who was only four feet, five inches tall. She was the nineteen-year-old daughter of Rueben Smith, one of his farm hands. Ruth was dark skinned, nice looking, and shapely, possessing tremendous sex appeal for her size. She made no attempt to hide her delight in GM, capitalizing on every opportunity to be in his view, especially at sunset.

GM hesitated at first, suppressing his lust, but his sexual passion finally crushed him. After supper one twilight, he took her for a walk near the wood line. She got pregnant by him in July. He immediately married her. She was immensely happy.

Without adequate prenatal care, Ruth suffered a stormy pregnancy, barely overcoming several threatened miscarriages. Near the end of gestation, she became seriously ill. No amount of treatment and care available to her in Vistula seemed to help. On April 1, 1902, Ruth and her baby died during her labor. Ruth and her child are buried in an unmarked grave in the all-black Vistula cemetery. Deeply remorseful, GM regretted his rash intercourse and marriage to Ruth, vowing never again to offend God by fornication or adultery.

The Shuffer and Butler farms were about five miles apart on opposite ends of Vistula, which by 1902 had been annexed by Lovelady, Texas. This small east Texas town, settled mostly by whites, together with Vistula, now formed the typical white burg

9

George Macon "GM" Shuffer, Sr. c. 1930.

with black suburb pattern of most locales in the South, indeed, in the North Midwest, and Western sections of the U.S. as well.

Sheriff John Bruton, owner of the thousand-acre Bruton Farm, started his drive to monopolize agricultural production and marketing in Houston County. He offered attractive prices to small farm owners in the region to sell their holdings to him. Many white and black owners sold out to Bruton, making his the controlling "plantation" in the county. Most black laborers (some former owners) in the area now worked for Bruton. Small, independent farmers began to starve for capable hands in a now scarce labor market. The Shuffer and Butler farms, along with those of seven other black owners, began to decline, but they stayed independent.

In September 1902, GM entered Prairie View Normal in pursuit of a business degree. Midway during his first semester, his progress and conduct reports were superior. Then one day he loaned Lonell Thigpen, a fellow freshman, ten dollars. Thigpen promised on oath to repay the loan plus one dollar in a week. A month passed without his paying. In the style of his father, GM proceeded to take his money from Thigpen by force. In the ensuing scuffle, GM took eleven dollars from Thigpen, leaving him prostrate with a bleeding nose and two black eyes. When Thigpen regained consciousness he vowed revenge.

A week later, as GM descended the dormitory stairs holding the right banister at the bottom step, Thigpen jumped from hiding under the staircase and with a fire poker, struck GM across his right eye and cheek bones, knocking the eye from its socket. Thigpen fled the scene. GM was rushed to the college infirmary for treatment. That night Thigpen slipped away from Prairie View never to return. It took almost two years for GM to get his cheek bone repaired, but he never found an eye to fill the empty socket.

Lying on his recovery bed, GM regretted his anger and violent rage in taking his money from Thigpen and beating him with his fists in the process. He begged God's forgiveness, but detested losing his right eye; yet, he realized that he deserved the injury and worse for breaking the law to have his way. It would have been better had he forgotten the ten dollars and continued his college study. Instead, Prairie View suspended him for a year, and GM never returned. Thigpen got expelled, but he could not be found to receive his sentence.

Early in 1906, GM, with a black patch strapped over his missing eye, healed sufficiently to retake management of the farm. During his absence from the helm, production had dropped by 70 percent. Many implements and tools were lost through theft and neglect. Garfield left shortly after GM went off to Prairie View, presumably in search of better employment in Anderson County. All hired hands, except Rueben Smith, deserted to Bruton Farm for higher pay. Livestock herds had thinned to a dangerously low level from reckless sales to offset plummeting crop profits and mounting debt. Waymon, now sixteen, and Survive, eleven, were incapable of effective management. Garfield returned when he got news of GM's injury, but it was his failure to find a better life that really caused him to come back.

GM and all in the family, including Fannie, worked fiercely, cutting spending to the bone, to restore production to former levels, but they could not arrest the decline. The heyday it seemed was gone forever. GM needed experienced laborers and substantial capital to rebuild his herds and increase production. Bruton stood in the way. His monopoly of the labor market, control of prices, and power of persuasion over Lovelady banks to deny loans to competitors (especially to blacks) put his plantation firmly in command of the agricultural market in Houston County. Reverting to conditions much like slavery days, smaller, independent farms were relegated to little more than subsistence entities, sustaining only immediate family and friends.

Since his high school days, GM had dreamed of establishing a general store in Vistula, preferably near the white/black community separating line of Lovelady. He visualized selling merchandise to black and white customers at competitive prices. Many householders of both communities customarily traveled to Crockett, almost twenty miles away, for necessary commodities obtainable in Lovelady only at Bruton's high prices.

In January 1908, Jeremiah Shandler, real estate broker and vice president of the Crockett State Bank, launched an enterprise to purchase Houston County acreage with potentially valuable subterranean minerals for investment. GM convinced Fannie to let him sell 250 acres of the farm for fifty dollars per acre. With the proceeds, he could establish the Shuffer General Store, fully stocked to realize quick profits and growth. Garfield, Waymon, and Survine all liked the idea. Near the month's end, GM closed the deal with Shandler Enterprises and began construction of his store.

The Shuffers rejoiced to see GM's dream materialize.

Compared with the aggressive Shuffers, the Butler family lived less ambitious, humbler lives. They were uniformly sanguine and accommodative to circumstances and conditions. Will and Ida, with seven sons and four daughters, were a cohesive, self-contained group, living on a farm half the size of the Shuffers'. They saw no need of outside laborers to achieve their goals. Bruton's exclusive control of agricultural production dented their potential, but did not threaten their expectations. They were satisfied with their means and possessions, and did not hesitate to share them with the poor. They were faithful members of the all-black Union Grove Baptist Church in Vistula. Ida worked with the missionary society and Sunday School, while Will helped the community where he could. He was a loyal member of Water Proof Lodge Number 225, Prince Hall Masons, black and strictly segregated from white masonry, as are Negro Masons to this day. He also prayed regularly with his family at home.

GM, Fannie, and Survine also attended worship service at Union Grove, and GM, after recovering from his injury, joined Water Proof Masonic Lodge. Garfield and Waymon rarely attended church.

It was at Union Grove where GM first noticed Johnnie Butler, five years his junior. She was thirteen and growing into a beautiful, shapely woman, with intelligent eyes and a ready smile. GM admired her, but he did not give her serious thought until she graduated from the county school system at eighteen in 1906. When he opened his general store in May 1908, he hired Johnnie as his store clerk.

Since she was a little girl, Johnnie had held GM in high esteem, longing for his attention and admiration. Even with one

Johnnie D'Ella Butler c. 1906.

Union Grove Baptist Church—Vistula.

eye, GM sported high appeal. In fact, as his store clerk, seeing him every day, her feelings of endearment towards him leaped higher. They fell in love and announced their intended marriage date, which they kept: July 15, 1908. They got their license in Crockett and went to Union Grove where Pastor George Walker married them in a service preceding a joyous reception at the Shuffer Farm. The Shuffer and Butler families have lived as one family in heart and spirit ever since.

Shuffer's farm, now half its original size, was easier to manage. Garfield, Waymon, and Survine, with Fannie's help, kept it producing. GM, although busy with his store, still lent a hand at the farm.

In 1911, while breaking in a newly acquired riding horse, the horse at full gallop, with GM in the saddle, fell and rolled. GM suffered a compound fracture of his left femur near the hip joint. Doctors had trouble fixing a splint to his hip and leg. It took almost a year for GM to walk with crutches. Then his stress and pain demanded surgery to re-break the fracture to obtain a better setting. It was near the end of 1913 before GM was able to walk without aids; then he did so with a noticeable rocking limp, because his left leg was permanently one and a half inches shorter than his right. Almost everyone snidely called him the "one-eyed limping dude." But GM lost little of his energy and drive to excel at what he did. He continued to run his store and help on the farm.

Nineteen hundred and fourteen saw him win the bid on a contract for a United States post office in his store to serve Vistula residents. Johnnie qualified to manage the post office as postmistress. Survine helped with the post and in the store as clerk.

Some friendly whites living close to the store desired to use the post office and shop at the store, but the local Klan immediately threatened GM and all whites in Lovelady with dire consequences if any white person entered his store. Only petty transactions could be made with whites (many were) surreptitiously outside the building, or by delivering merchandise free of transit charge to back doors of white homes. GM's store's attraction and success now began to stir white animosity against the

Shuffers to levels reminiscent of their farm heyday. Even newly elected Sheriff Robert Zimmerman and some Lovelady policemen (suspected of being secret members of the KKK) increased their surveillance of the store.

Compounding the suspicion and hatred of the Shuffers was Waymon's aberrant behavior. Among Jacob's sons, Waymon inherited the lion's share of his white hatred. He went out of his way to leer and scowl at whites whom he perceived were giving him dirty looks and often engaged in fisticuffs with them. Then too, he would often slip away secretly to gamble with a select group of rowdy white teens, playing dice and cards. He was exceptionally skilled and cunning at gambling, winning most of his bets. Even when he lost, the games usually ended in a fight. His quickness and strength generally overwhelmed his opponents. Most feared him, and refused to fight. Others, choosing to stand their ground, came away angry losers. Just before Christmas, Waymon married Leathanne Jackson and started a family. His rowdiness tempered somewhat, but he was never able to resist temptation to fight whites.

GM bought a brand new Model T Ford sedan one autumn day in October. Johnnie and all in the household, except Fannie, got a license to drive. But Johnnie was depressed and disappointed over her inability to carry a pregnancy to term. She conceived seven times since her marriage, and each time she lost the embryo in miscarriage. She and GM grieved sorrowfully in their frustration. They visited doctors in Lovelady and Crockett, but none could discover the cause, nor prescribe a cure. They began praying constantly for children and pleaded with church members at Union Grove to pray for them.

When Johnnie got pregnant in January 1915, she quietly rejoiced with a certain feeling this time a healthy baby would come, and come he did, Jacob Mirjan, born October 18. Thirteen months later, Bernice Alfrez arrived, adding another healthy son. Johnnie forgot her fears of being a barren wife and thanked God for His gifts, while continuing to ask for more children.

When the United States prepared to enter the First World War in 1917, Congress passed the Selective Service Act in May. The measure required all men between the ages of twenty-one

Waymon M. Shuffer c. 1914.

and thirty (later, eighteen and forty-five) to register for military service. Those registered were divided into five classes, the first of which consisted of able-bodied, unmarried men, without dependents. Most of the men actually selected for service came from this category alone. All the Shuffer and Butler men registered. Only Survine Shuffer and Luther Butler qualified in the first class.

Survine got picked in January 1918. After basic training, he was deployed with the all-black Ninety-second Infantry Division to the ports of Normandy in France. The division mainly performed theater reserve security and stevedore details. Survine served as a mail clerk in the postal section of the 366th Infantry Regiment headquarters.

Luther Butler was drafted in late summer 1918. By the time he completed basic training and joined a unit still in the States, the war ended. Both Survine and Luther were discharged and returned home before Christmas. World War I and its aftermath caused mild inflation, but it had little other adverse economic effect in rural east Texas.

Waymon, however, was the catalyst that terminated the Shuffers', and to a large extent, the Butlers' stay in Houston County. His rough behavior and habitual gambling, previously undisclosed and kept in private circles, leaked to others in Lovelady, including the Klan. Unaware of the leak, he pressed on.

On Saturday afternoon, August 19, 1917, Waymon accompanied Fannie and Garfield to Lovelady in the family car. They went to pay bills and buy medicine from the drug store. Waymon slipped off with his gaming gang to shoot dice and play cards. Consistent, he got into a fight with two whites, new to the group and armed with switch blades. Waymon also carried a knife. In the clash, Waymon stabbed one seriously in the shoulder and almost severed the left hand at the wrist of the other. He ran off and hid until dark when he joined Fannie and Garfield at the car.

Together they started home; Garfield driving, Waymon in the right front seat, and Fannie in the back seat. Along the FM road home just past a bend, several Klansmen, armed with shot-

Survine Sewell Shuffer c. 1929.

Luther N. Butler c. 1920.

guns, had set an ambush. The ambush party laid a pile of tree limbs across the road sufficient to block a car's passage. Garfield stopped at the obstacle with headlights burning, and Waymon got out to remove it. In the glare of the headlights, Waymon was an easy target for the shotgun volley that took his life. Garfield quickly turned off the lights, but a second blast at the car in the dark wounded him in the right shoulder. Fannie was not hit. Garfield jumped out of the car and hid in the bushes opposite the ambush side of the road. Fannie crouched on the floor. After checking to see that Waymon was dead, those in the ambuscade departed the area.

On a nearby farm, a black family heard the shots and cautiously approached the site. Ascertaining that the ambushers had gone, they rushed in to render aid to Garfield's wounds and put Waymon's body in the car. They cleared away the obstacle and took them home to the Shuffer farm.

The following Tuesday, after Waymon's funeral, Sheriff Zimmerman and the Chief of Lovelady police warned GM, the remaining Shuffers, and Will Butler that they could no longer provide safety for them or any in their families anywhere in Houston County. They strongly urged them to leave the county permanently within ninety days. This confirmed GM's and Will's suspicion that most, if not all, law-enforcement officials in the county were indeed members of the Ku Klux Klan, sworn to carry out its thug agenda.

What could the victim do? No higher authority (except God, the source of all authority and power) would dare countermand or redress the wrongs done, or confront the unjust, illegal "order," coercing them to "run for their lives" from the county, at least none GM or Will could trust. So they prayed, while preparing to comply.

GM went to his friend Jeremiah Shandler in Crockett and negotiated the sale of his store, stock and all, to Shandler Enterprises. The sum he got is unknown, but he claimed to have gotten a decent profit from the sale. Fannie and GM left their farm in the care of Lee Halley, GM's deceased sister Pearley's husband. Fannie, Garfield, GM, and Survine moved to Palestine, Texas. Leathanne, and Casel, Waymon's only legitimate child, went to

22

live in Marlin, Texas. Before the end of 1917, Will and Ida moved to a farm north of Palestine near Montalba, Texas. All the other Butlers, except Jay and Fay, the younger of the children, left for various points in Texas. Jay and Fay remained on the farm on constant alert.

It was a shameful, angry time for Negroes in Lovelady/Vistula. They silently mourned Waymon's death and the Shuffer and Butler departures, but they managed to stay the course, prayerfully begging for the day when Klan terrorism would end. Hateful whites rejoiced. They had virtually achieved their goal to rid the county of Shuffers and most of the Butlers. Racial tension remained high in the county until United States involvement in World War II.

2

Palestine, Texas

The Shuffers found Palestine larger with more brick buildings and paved streets than Lovelady/Vistula, but little different socially and economically. It had a population of 10,890 (blacks making up one-third) and is the seat of Anderson County. Having red clay soil, stately pines, pin oaks, and sycamores, it sits between the Neeches and Trinity Rivers, 100 miles southeast of Dallas and 125 miles north of Houston. Its unique dogwood trees, with blossoms smaller, but as brilliant and white as magnolias, form a trail through Palestine's countryside. In full bloom at midspring, they attract tourists nationwide. Modern-day festivals, featuring runs and chili cook-offs, excluding blacks of course, lend excitement to an otherwise drab locale.

Black-town Palestine (old town) lies south and east of the Missouri Pacific Railroad tracks, which transects the city on a northeast/southwest axis. A smaller group of black families spills over the railroad tracks northwesterly, pushing population growth toward the Freestone County line.

GM and Johnnie bought 1305 West Carolina Street, a three and a half acre lot with an unpainted three-room (two bedrooms, a kitchen, and side porch) house and a large barn. They liked the place because it had a large garden area, and the barn could stall three cows. It also had an acre of grazing pasture across a stream behind the garden, which could sustain five cows.

Carolina Street traversed northern Palestine, which was "white town." Ours was one of five black families living on the street. These were on contiguous lots (north side of street) separated from whites on the street by a string of unoccupied lots measuring five hundred yards flanking each side. We were essentially an enclave of the segregated who got no different treat-

24

ment, in the main, than Negroes on the south side. This setting, however, of a few blacks living in close proximity to whites, gave instances and opportunities for neighborly contact and communication, engendering better understanding and respect than larger groups of the races similarly juxtaposed enjoyed. White families with children, especially Thomas Shade's, with seven kids, let their children play and make friends with us, and their parents expressed concern for our welfare. In fact, all of the white families near us on the street got friendlier as time passed.

Fannie stayed with GM. Garfield moved to the south side, taking the job of janitor at the post office. Survine, discharged from war service after Armistice Day, moved to Chicago and became a clerk in its post office.

GM helped Johnnie and Fannie cultivate a bountiful garden of beans, tomatoes, black-eyed peas, potatoes, squash, cabbage, collard greens, and okra. They also set in some peach and pear trees, and revived several languishing blackberry bushes along the back fence. He also bought three milk cows, a flock of setting hens, and a rooster.

McKnight Plaza (affectionately called the "Square") contained all the black-owned businesses in Palestine. It sat in the extreme southeast corner downtown. There was the Farmers and Citizens State Bank, a café, grocery store, barber shop, drug store, and two physicians' offices. Two black dentists maintained offices in their homes.

The Missouri Pacific Hospital was the only health care facility where Negroes could receive service, and that was on a limited basis, as only Missouri Pacific employees and their dependents were admitted. Black physicians took their patients out of town for surgery. Prairie View Normal's hospital, 145 miles away, was the recipient of many Colored patients from Palestine.

Small town retail, wholesale, and agriculture constituted the city's economic base. The Missouri Pacific Railway maintained a switching yard, turn table, and rail car shed in town. It was the closest thing to an "industry" anywhere in the county. White employees of the rail line received good pay; blacks, confined to Red Cap and porter jobs, were paid the black middle income rate. The two Negro physicians, the dentists, and the bank president comprised the affluent class of black Palestine, averaging incomes of fifty dollars a month. Middle-income Coloreds (getting fifteen to thirty dollars per month) included schoolteachers, church pastors, business owners, funeral directors (two in town), and Red Caps and porters working for the railroad. GM, after he established his dry goods store, was among this group. The rest of the Coloreds labeled "poor" were farmers and domestic servants of whites who made two dollars or less per week. By 1940, when I left to join the army, black income overall had averaged a gradual rise of forty percent.

Comparatively, whites in all income categories bettered blacks by forty or more percent. White schoolteachers, for example, got fifty to eighty dollars a month in 1917. Statistics of white schoolteacher qualifications vis-à-vis black in the period are not available. Of the sixteen black schoolteachers in Palestine, only four had college degrees. Many of the others had varying amounts of college experience. Some had none. [N.B. Despite these "apparent" deficiencies among black teacher qualifications, those responsible for my formation were excellent to superior. In fact, graduates of Palestine's black schools after 1920 hold comparatively good records overall qualifying for college or employment. The problem was and is that opportunities to pursue post high school graduation endeavors were not equally available to blacks. I give credit for my formation and qualifications to my teachers and principals, who did a super job preparing me for life after graduation.]

Jim Crow laws and traditions segregated blacks in every aspect of life. Domestic servants were excepted while serving in white homes. Yet, they had to enter and depart the home only via the back door. When shopping in any white-operated business, Negroes stood back (males with heads uncovered), deferring to white customers needing help. White cafés and restaurants, if they served blacks at all, fed them through the kitchen back door.

Two each all-black Baptist and Methodist churches provided places of Protestant worship. The few Catholics of color went to Sacred Heart Church for Mass, utilizing the back pew marked "Coloreds Only." For Holy Communion, all white communicants received first and returned to their pews before blacks could approach. Warning signs posted in the church threatened police closure, if the pastor failed to enforce these rules. There were no known black Jews or Muslims in Palestine.

Negro children went to all-black public schools (three elementary, one high school) using handed-down textbooks studied by white students for two or more years. The antiquated science laboratory at Lincoln High restricted teaching to only the basic, introductory approaches to science, and school libraries were non-existent.

Movie houses (called "theaters" in Palestine) sat blacks in their balconies. Coloreds could ride only the back seats of buses and the "coal cinder" car of trains (the one immediately attached to the engine). One black taxi driver was available to Negroes. White cab drivers would not ride blacks.

And so it was. Two starkly separated races with no chance of meaningful colloquy to foster mutual understanding and respect. No wonder distrust, suspicion, fear, and hatred prevailed. Little hope for improvement of these conditions found room in the hearts and minds of whites or blacks. Practically everyone, before United States involvement in World War II, grew complacent with their situations, seemingly finding comfort only in egotistical indifference. Police and Klansmen enforced these laws and traditions. At times ordinary white citizens angrily kept blacks in line, confident of police backup.

Early in 1919, GM established his dry goods store in a vacant building in the Square. His and all the black-owned enterprises in the complex thrived, because their prices were competitive, and Negroes could shop with dignity.

Johnnie was happy to be pregnant in April 1918. Fannie Estelle, her first girl, came premature in December. She lived until February; then died of influenza, a dreadful virus that took a heavy toll of Texans in 1919. Johnnie also was afflicted, but she recovered after a lengthy illness. She rejoiced to be pregnant again that autumn.

When Eunice Juanette came on May 20, 1920, Johnnie and GM thanked God for another healthy, strong child, and kept praying for more children. She was blessed with another strong, joyful girl. Willetta Louise, born February 21, 1922, reassured her of the wholeness of her potential for having children. But GM and Johnnie did not stop there. She conceived and gave birth to George Macon, Jr., September 27, 1923. I, too, was a healthy child. They continued their struggle to have more children throughout Johnnie's child-bearing years, but without success.

Midwife Jane Donnell delivered me, but she recorded my name incorrectly. She listed me: *Wm Macon Shuffel* and Johnnie's maiden name was wrongly spelled *Butter*. Jane was illiterate and a heavy snuff dipper. With a large wad of snuff in her lower lip, she had difficulty pronouncing words, especially names, to the recording clerk. GM was alone in his store that day and relied on Jane to register me. I did not get the record corrected until October 14, 1964.

Palestine School District had no preschool or kindergarten programs before 1940. Children were admitted to first grade at age five. I became so attached to Willetta during my preschool years that I demanded to accompany her to first grade in September 1927 when she turned five. I was an "old" three.

Washington Elementary was three quarters of a mile from home via quiet dirt roads. There were no school buses. I persuaded Johnnie to arrange with first-grade teacher Thompson to let me "audit" the grade, if she had room and I would not interfere with her teaching. She agreed; so I walked with Willetta to school everyday, carrying a sack lunch, pencil, and writing tablet, careful to listen only. When I entered first grade, September 5, 1928, twenty-two days before my fifth birthday, I had a year's head start and familiarity with learning in school.

Up to age nine, I enjoyed a satisfactory standard of living. The roaring economy of the North during the 1920s trickled down abundantly to east Texas. Wages inched up while prices remained stable. Clothing styles changed; and GM's business thrived. He bought a used 1929 Studebaker four-door sedan in 1930, making us one of the few black families in town owning a car. He also bought two more cows, a donkey, and plows to deep-cultivate the garden.

One cold night in January 1931, the potbellied stove in the

GM's and Johnnie's children: Alfrez, Willetta, Jacob, Eunice, and George, Jr. October 30, 1974.

bedroom where Fannie, Eunice, Willetta, and I slept, over-heated, setting afire the wall paper. In minutes the old, un-painted structure burst into full flame. Everyone in the house fled to safety in their nightclothes. The neighbors brought quilts, and the family took refuge in the barn, which escaped fire dam-age. Many prayers of thanksgiving for our safety followed. The nearest white family with a telephone was Tom Shade's, who called the fire station when they noticed the blaze. GM thanked them, too, but the fire engine did not arrive at the site until the building was only a pile of hot coals and ashes.

Our barn had three split-level hay lofts with sufficient hay to mattress the floors. It also had a garage opposite the cow stalls, which served as kitchen, sitting, and dining rooms. GM rented a kerosene stove, tables, chairs, and lamps. Neighbors (some white) loaned us cooking and chinaware and utensils. We removed the cows, wagon, and garden tools, and occupied the barn as the family domicile until a new home could be built.

It was the middle of April before GM could get construction started on a new home. They dug out a basement, lined it with cement, and installed a furnace with a water-bearing belt around its middle and warm air ducts extending to every room in the house. Opportunely, city water had just finished laying lines to all residents on Carolina; so plumbers modernized the build-ing with hot and cold running water in the kitchen and bath. The furnace in the basement distinguished the dwelling as the only black-owned home in Anderson County with central heating. Builders completed the house for occupancy in June.

It had four bedrooms, a bath, living and dining rooms, kitchen, a screened back porch, and a front porch with installed swing. Cost: $3,500, which GM paid through a twenty-year mort-gage agreement. The bathroom with hot and cold running water, porcelain tub, flush toilet, and electric lights so fascinated Willetta and me (the other children, too) that we each took seven baths the first occupancy day. This "bath opulence" was indeed a long way from the drudgery of the twenty-five-foot-deep back yard well, number-three tin tub, kerosene lantern, and out-house. Before, GM and Johnnie had to take us kicking and screaming to our mandatory weekly bath.

30

First, High First, and Second grades—Washington Elementary School, September, 1927. Teacher, Martha Thompson (upper right, back row). Left arrow points to George, Jr., right arrow to Wiletta.

1305 West Carolina Street, 1976 (temporarily unoccupied).

Then came the 1933 Depression, which hit with the force of an economic blackout. Abject poverty replaced the little prosperity that Palestine had enjoyed before. It wiped out GM's business, leaving him broke and nearly bankrupt. The all-black Farmers and Citizens Bank, holding his assets, failed. He had to sell all his goods for one-fifth their value; his car went for less than half its original cost. He sold four of his cows and thanked God for his bountiful garden and flock of chickens.

GM subsequently rented a forty-acre farm on the edge of town for twenty-five dollars a year, which provided us a marginal existence during the remainder of the thirties and most of the forties. Johnnie sold butter and eggs, while taking in home laundry of whites to help pay off mounting debt. Our living standard and lifestyle dropped dismally low. With the store gone, new clothes for us children were reduced to dreams. Leisure and play time vanished. Every moment out of school saw us working on the farm, in the garden, and washing and ironing "white folks" laundry. We prayed perseveringly for relief, but this came painfully slow.

Some of the relief, recovery, and reform measures of Presidents Herbert Hoover and Franklin Roosevelt dribbled down to Palestine, but not with sufficient speed and quantity to produce meaningful reform or recovery. It would require much patience, hard work, and time.

Fortuitously for me, at this low point of our impoverishment, my Sunday school class at West Union Baptist was studying the story of Job in the Scriptures. I awoke spiritually, impressed by Job's lament: "Naked I came forth from my mother's womb, and naked I shall go back again. The Lord gave and the Lord has taken away; blessed be the name of the Lord!" (Job 1:21–22). Job's life example taught me that no matter how bad and tough life becomes, if I held fast to faith, hope, and trust in the Lord, He would reward me with a much better existence later, as Job's life story attested. Hope and trust help us endure.

I received baptism on September 27, 1935 at West Union and graduated from Washington Elementary at the top of my class on June 8, 1936. For secondary education, I attended Lincoln High School, starting September 3. My favorite courses

33

were History, Geography, and Science. Mathematics gave me no trouble, but I never relished its study. I worked summers on the farm, while occasionally finding time to enjoy swimming and trumpet playing. Borrowing the band teacher's trumpet (GM never had the money to buy or rent one), I marched with Lincoln High's band and played second trumpet in the school orchestra. Never excelling with the trumpet, due to lack of natural talent and practice time, I kept trying and got better through the years. I graduated as valedictorian from Lincoln on June 6, 1940.

Graduating as valedictorian brought me one-year academic scholarships to the following colleges (all black): Mary Allen Junior College, Crockett, Texas; Lemoyne College, Memphis, Tennessee; and Lincoln University near Philadelphia, Pennsylvania. I delayed going to college. My parents were too poor to pay room and board and fees necessary above tuition, which the scholarship covered. No meaningful jobs were available to me in Palestine, and the colleges offering scholarships had no positions for me to "work" my way even through the first semester. My two older sisters were attending Prairie View, and the home mortgage was on the brink of foreclosure. [GM adhered to the philosophy: "In hard times, educate daughters in preference to sons; so, in case that they are unable to find suitable partners to marry, they will be prepared to provide for themselves. Sons: 'Fend for yourselves!' "]

Jacob completed his freshman year at Bishop College and part of his sophomore before the Depression took hold. He and Alfrez, disappointed and desperate in their search for employment, joined the army in 1935 to ease the family's financial crisis. They were so destitute that they traveled on freight trains as transients, hoboes, riding from Palestine to Hereford, Arizona, and hitchhiked to Fort Huachuca to join the army there. They sent allotment checks of five dollars each per month. I decided, if necessary, to do the same after high school graduation, and join the army, too, and help with an allotment of my pay.

My father strongly objected, saying: "The army will corrupt you and turn you into a beast; besides, I need you to help on the farm." Even with tearful pleading, I could not get GM's approval. Johnnie, on the other hand, confidentially agreed to help me en-

34

Lincoln High School Graduating Class, June, 1940.

Top Row, L-R: Rosa Nell Thompson, Gloria Lee Irving, Goldie Faye Manning, Georgie Holbert, Irma Mathis, Mary Belle Reed, Thelma Clevis, Johnnie Mae Tatum, Gloria Robinson, Johnnie Mae Stevenson, Geneva Collins, Thelma Chester, Vergil Berry, Ida Mae Coleman, Grace Owens.

Center Row, L-R: Willie J. Andy, Homer Ruben, Ernest Marshall, Claud White, Dimp Payne, George Macon Shuffer, Jr., E. W. Henry, Booker T. Davis, S. E. Freeman, Vergil Keeton, Harold Register, Lee Aurther Jenkins, Mr. Cyde Gillespie (Science Teacher).

First Row, L-R: Ada Lee Henry, Hallie McClure, Louie Cummings, Lucelle Jackson, Maurice Anderson, Bernice Anderson, Louise Beard, Ethelyne Smith, Mildred Allen, Earlie Mae Nixson, Ethelle Beets, Dorothy Bailey, Flora Dean Taylor, Helen Swanson.

ter the army, reasoning it would be better than anything in Palestine. After much prayer and soul-searching, I decided with Johnnie's concurrence to slip away from home without GM knowing. It would take careful planning and confidential coordination.

Before 1948 the army was racially segregated. Whites served in all-white units; blacks in all-black outfits, which consisted of Negro enlisted men and white commissioned officers, except perhaps the chaplain and a specialty warrant officer (band leader or administrative technician) who could be Negroid.

In summer 1940, the black army had two infantry regiments (Twenty-fourth and Twenty-fifth), two calvary regiments (Ninth and Tenth, which were phased out)—the touted "Buffalo Soldier" units—and a quartermaster company. Federal budget constraints limited these components to personnel strengths two-thirds their authorized levels. Thus, a regiment normally with three battalions could have only two active. The other battalion was imaginary for training purposes. Even active elements could not exceed sixty-five percent of normal personnel strength.

In June that year, the Twenty-fifth Infantry at Fort Huachuca, Arizona, afforded Negroes their only opportunity to enlist. Other black units had no enlistment quotas. This dictated travel to the remote post to become a soldier. I figured it would take at least twenty-five dollars to pay bus and train fare, plus subsistence during the day and half of travel. Johnnie had no money; so short of "hoboing" or hitch-hiking, I needed a loan to get there. Additionally, I had to keep secret my departure, i.e., slip away. Johnnie planned to cover my escape as best she could.

Mrs. Cora Scott, a domestic servant for a white family on nearby Esplanade Street, was renting a room in our house for one dollar a week. She was the wife of a church minister who had become insane and confined to the Rusk, Texas, Insane Asylum. Her wages were three dollars per week plus meals. Week after week, she invariably paid Johnnie the dollar rent; then stuffed the other two in a snuff can (she was an avid snuff dipper) already bulging with dollar bills. The dollar-overfilled can immediately joined several others, equally loaded with bills, under her bed pillow.

I knew it would take an inordinate length of time for Johnnie to accumulate the twenty-five dollars needed, so I chanced asking Mrs. Scott for a loan; without hesitation, she obliged, carefully peeling the crumpled bills from the cans, while counting them aloud as she pressed out the wrinkles.

Mother overheard the counting and rushed to assure Cora free rent for twenty-five weeks, if I did not repay the loan in four months. She also took her into confidence not to reveal the transaction to GM.

I had the chore of milking the cows at 5:00 A.M. every day. After securing the milk in the ice box, I herded the cows to a new grazing pasture (county property that GM arranged to use) a mile away. It was adjacent to Highway 19 to Dallas. A Trailways bus to Dallas passed along the highway daily at 7:00 A.M. I decided to catch that bus to Dallas; then go by train to Hereford, Arizona, which sat in a valley a short bus-hop distance up the mountain to Huachuca.

My brother, Private First Class Jacob M. Shuffer, Headquarters Company, Twenty-fifth Infantry at Huachuca, visited home on June 1st en route to a three-week radio communications course at Fort Benning, Georgia. Jacob agreed to meet me, as he would be returning through Dallas after his course ended, on the same train that I planned to catch on June 27. The train's 2:00 P.M. departure from Dallas to Huachuca (Hereford) would allow an easy connection for me, if I caught the 7:00 A.M. bus from Palestine. Jacob and I could then travel together to my army entry point.

On June 27th, I executed the plan precisely. GM discovered my escape about the same time I was catching the flagged bus on Highway 19. I had stowed my "get away" bag (a paper sack) under the porch of one of Tom Shade's married daughters' home, which was near the entrance to the grazing pasture.

GM immediately wrote a letter to the commanding officer of the Twenty-fifth, asking him to refuse my enlistment because I was under age eighteen and did not have his permission to enter the army. He also requested that the commander turn me over to the police for lock-up until he could arrange to escort my return home. He knew this latter plea was beyond the officer's power and authority to give. He was simply venting his anger and outrage at my disobedience and disrespect.

Penning the letter before breakfast, he slammed it into the mail box in front of the house and angrily jammed up the alert flag. After breakfast he mounted his donkey and rode off to the farm. On the way he stopped by the police station to report me missing.

Mail pickup occurred at 11:00 A.M. When GM left on his donkey, Johnnie took the letter from the box and enclosed it in an envelope addressed to me c/o of Jacob's address. She also enclosed a formal letter to the commander authorizing me to join the army over her signature: "The Parents."

I ate a "Mr. Goodbar" for breakfast after dismounting at the railway station in Dallas. Not long after 11:30 A.M., I saw Jacob in the window of the "coal cinder" car of the train creeping to a halt on the arrival track. We got a hamburger for lunch from the kitchen of a nearby restaurant and prepared for 2:00 P.M. departure.

3
Enlisted Service

Jacob and I arrived at Huachuca's Brown Field, Friday, June 28, just as an impressive retreat parade began. My face flushed, seeing almost two thousand sharply dressed soldiers with glistening rifles marching to some of the tunes that I played at Lincoln High. The bus stopped in front of Headquarters and Service Company building, a newly constructed barracks, where I would stay until Mother's authorization letter arrived.

After the parade, I enjoyed supper in the troop mess hall. We ate bountiful portions family style around twelve-man tables, served by dining room orderlies. These worked in choice positions on the kitchen police (KP) detail won in weekly competition for the "better soldier" award. Others on the KP detail did the kitchen dirty work. With supper over, Jacob drew clean linens for me from the supply room and got me a bunk close to his in the barracks bay area. So, favorably impressed with this reception by the army, I struggled to think at all about Palestine.

On Sunday, I went to Protestant worship in the post chapel wearing my brother's only civilian suit. Jacob did not attend the service. There at the chapel I saw Cecilia Rose Mann, who was playing the piano for the service. I did not meet her then, but our eyes met, and lingered; that was enough! Never before had I seen a girl so beautiful and talented. She was in high school, living with her parents, Sergeant Jesse R. Mann, her stepfather, and her mother Maria, on post. I found out later that she and her family were Catholics. She was retained only to play music for Protestant services. I also learned a sketchy outline of her family's background.

Edward A. Rose, born the son of a white, small farm owner in West Point, Mississippi, in 1864, was Cecilia's grandfather on

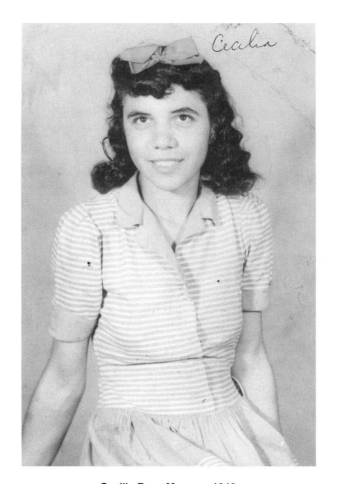

Cecilia Rose Mann, c. 1940.

her father's side. He studied law at the University of Mississippi at Oxford and began a practice in West Point in 1890. He fathered Raymond M. Rose, Cecilia's father, by his black housekeeper and cook, Eulalia "Lula" Jones, in January 1892.

Raymond grew up and finished high school in West Point before selection for military service in 1918. After basic training, he went to the Twenty-fifth Infantry and spent the war mounting guard patrols in Hawaii. Two battalions of the regiment had the same duty in the Philippines. After the war in 1919, Raymond's unit returned to Camp Stephen D. Little at Nogales, Arizona, along the Mexican border.

Sergeant Jesse R. Mann came to birth in July 1895 and grew up in Washington, D.C. He enlisted in 1916 before the Selective Service Act was passed. After basic, he joined the newly organized all-black, except for commissioned officers, 92nd Infantry Division and was deployed to France with the 365th Infantry in 1918. The regiment participated in some skirmishes, but mostly handled supply route security and stevedore duties. When the war ended, the 92nd returned to the States for immediate deactivation. Private Mann went to the 25th unit on the U.S./Mexico border at Camp Little.

Born March 28, 1901 in Tepic, Nayarit, Mexico, Maria Encarnacion Flores, Cecilia's mother, migrated to Nogales, Sonora, Mexico, in 1919. In truth, she was running scared with her family for safety in or near the United States.

After the fall of President Porfiro Diaz in 1910, Mexico lived in the throes of revolution for ten years. Several revolutionary factions led by strongmen vied for the presidency in a series of military coups and assassinations. Beginning with Francisco Madero in 1910, followed by Victoriano Huerta, and Venustiano Carranza, who finally gained full recognition by the United States as President in 1915. He was strongly opposed by Francisco "Pancho" Villa, whose revolutionary faction controlled large areas of Mexico. Villa's forceful recruiting of men and boys to swell his fighting ranks directly threatened males of the Flores family in Tepic. They were: Alvino Sr., Cecilia's grandfather; Alvino Jr., and Tomas, her uncles.

Rafaela Moran de Flores, Cecilia's grandmother, dressed

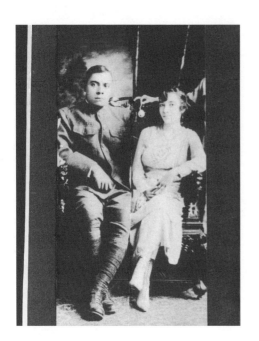

Pfc. Raymond M. Rose and
Maria E. Flores after marriage,
July 1919.

Pfc. Jesse R. Mann, c. 1919.

Maria Encarnacion Flores, c. 1919.

Alvino Jr. and Tomas as girls and fled with Michaela, Maria, and Angela, her daughters, north along Mexico's Highway 15 to Nogales (the Mexican side of the border). Alvino Sr. chose to stay in Tepic and continue managing Tepic's only slaughter house, hoping to avoid Villa's draft. He did escape service with Villa and remained in Tepic with his meat-cutting business.

When Rafaela and children arrived in Nogales, she purchased a home and went to work in Baldarama Laundry and Garment factory. She, Michaela, and Maria were masterful seamstresses; so they all were employed by Baldarama. Alvino Jr. went to work at Rivera's Slaughter House as a meat cutter. Angela and Tomas, ages nine and seven respectively, were enrolled in public schools.

Every Sunday afternoon, Mexican families loved to stroll, dine, and relax in the town plaza, while being entertained by Mariachi bands. Soldiers on pass from Camp Little routinely joined in the fun and pleasance. All in the Flores family were bilingual, speaking and writing English and Spanish.

Sunday, on March 9, 1919, Privates First Class Jesse R. Mann, a machine gun crew gunner, and Raymond M. Rose, an army cook, met Maria and her family in the plaza. Raymond and Jesse were buddies, and Maria was clearly the most beautiful and engaging of the Flores girls. Raymond and Jesse both courted Maria competitively until Jesse went back to Washington, D.C. to visit his sick mother on June 10th. Before he could return to vie more conclusively for Maria's heart, Raymond married her and made her a U.S. citizen. Michaela also married a soldier from the Twenty-fifth, acquired U.S. citizenship, but immediately abandoned him, taking a night train to Los Angeles. Maria, on the other hand, was happily married to Raymond and remained with him. They lived together in Raymond's small home in Nogales, Arizona. Not long after their marriage, however, the entire Flores family infiltrated to the U.S. side and took residence in Rose's house.

Meantime, Michaela got a job at the Diamond Queen Laundry in LA and began scouting jobs and living quarters for the Floreses to take in Los Angeles. By the end of 1919, the entire Flores family, except Maria, who remained in Nogales, had

45

Rafaela Moran de Flores with Cecilia, c. 1926.

moved to Los Angeles and found jobs and places to live. Angela and Tomas enrolled in LA's public schools.

Early the next year, Raymond applied for short discharge from the army and received approval for July 1920. He and Maria decided that Maria should go to LA immediately, obtain a job, and find a home for Raymond to buy. Raymond would stay on duty at Camp Little, finishing his enlistment and selling his Nogales home. When Maria got to LA, she started working at the Diamond Queen and began searching for a home. She chose 1630 East Jefferson Boulevard in south Los Angeles. On a short predischarge leave, Raymond closed purchase of the East Jefferson home and cleared sale of his Nogales residence.

When he arrived in LA, Rose opened a candy and ice cream store across the street from the Lincoln Theater. He was an expert cook and confection maker. His outstanding performance in the army as a cook propelled him to specialty ratings with comparative pay equal to sergeants. Now in his store, his near-perfect products made his business an instant success. He also bought two trucks for a short-haul transfer business. With his candy and ice cream store, his transfer business gave impetus to his success as an LA businessman.

Since their marriage, Maria had strived to have children, but without success. She consulted several physicians, who, like those Johnnie had seen, found no cause, and prescribed no remedy for her barrenness. Finally, in 1925, after much prayer, she got pregnant with Cecilia, who came on October 19, a healthy child. Two boys followed, David and Ramon Mario, December 25, 1927 and November 22, 1929, respectively, also healthy and fine.

Raymond and Maria were happy and thankful for their children, but Raymond was an inveterate gambler, practicing the habit that he developed during his military days. Many evenings, he would stay out all night, betting on anything he could persuade others to chance (he would even bet on the weather). Mostly he shot dice and played cards. His winnings were marvelous, but Maria was incensed. In fact, by 1931 his betting gambits so aggravated her contempt for his habit that she threatened to leave him.

Then one early January day in 1932, after a heated argu-

47

Raymond and Maria's children—David, Cecilia, and Mario, c. 1933.

ment, Raymond slapped Maria, leaving a swollen welt on her cheek. In disgust, he packed his clothes and left, taking residence somewhere across town. Maria immediately filed for divorce, which became final in March 1933.

Meanwhile, the Twenty-fifth Infantry had replaced the Tenth Cavalry as the main combat force at Fort Huachuca. The Twenty-fifth had been infiltrating small elements from Camp Little to Huachuca since 1929, anticipating army closure of the Nogales camp.

Corporal Mann moved from Little to Huachuca in 1929. He got word of Maria's divorce proceedings in summer 1932. He immediately renewed his acquaintance with her by correspondence. Maria's quick response deepened their affection for each other, which had begun that festival afternoon in the town plaza back in 1919. Jesse had not dated a girl since Maria married Raymond that year.

On a thirty-day leave, Jesse went to Los Angeles on May 31, 1933. He and Maria married on June 4th, and they departed for Huachuca with the children. Her divorce settlement with Raymond required him to pay each of the three children thirty-five dollars per month until they reached eighteen. Raymond kept the Jefferson Boulevard house. Jesse took his new family to residence on OK Street in Bisbee, Arizona (twenty-three miles from Huachuca), until he got quarters on post the week before Christmas.

I got Johnnie's letter with GM's enclosed on the Wednesday following my arrival at Huachuca. I destroyed my father's letter and cherished Mother's, for it helped me enlist. GM made no further efforts to block my entry into the army.

Regimental Sergeant Major Ora Saunders "attached" me to Company L, because recruiting quotas for June and July were already filled. *Attachment* meant one performed KP, barracks, and company area cleaning chores for food and shelter only, no pay! So I passed the physical and mental tests to become a soldier and did attachment duties until August quotas came.

Meanwhile, I spent every spare moment trying to meet and know more about Cecilia. Across the street from her high school sat Carnahan Hall, a gymnasium with band stage and new hardwood floors. Every Saturday night, it was converted to a dance hall, where the Twenty-fifth's orchestra played dance music until 10:00 P.M., mainly for high school students (Huachuca High had no band); but also for as many others, including soldiers, as the hall could hold, who came to dance. The post commander had standing orders forbidding soldiers to date or marry school girls. All girls under age eighteen, in school or not, had to be chaperoned either by their parents or a responsible adult. Tobacco and alcohol products were barred from the hall and from within a hundred yards of its surrounding area.

Maria brought Cecilia to dance practically every Saturday night. I met and danced with her every time I could during my six-month stay at Huachuca. I also would go every day possible to watch her roller skate (as she did for thirty minutes after school) with her brothers on the tennis court; then watch her walk home, following at a "safe" distance. It was sheer pleasure just seeing her. Dreams of running off with her to some hidden paradise, where I would never lose her touch, frolicked through my head. From the happy summer of 1940 until we married, we maintained intermittent contact by correspondence and occasional visits despite the long involuntary separation due to the war.

I enlisted on August 16, 1940 and took basic training from selected officers and noncommissioned officers (NCOs) in the regiment. Drill Sergeant H. "Muddy" Waters picked me as top soldier of my basic class and got me promoted to private first class at graduation. Designated acting corporal the same day, I trained newly inducted draftees in the regimental training area in Knoxville on the western edge of the post.

After paying my debt to Mrs. Scott, I regularly sent two-thirds of my pay home to Johnnie every month (twenty dollars as a Pfc). Subsequently, with every promotion, I did the same, until I married in 1946.

Orders transferring me with a training cadre to Camp Wolters, Mineral Wells, Texas, on February 1, 1941, sent me into a tizzy of dismay and distress. The transfer brought promotion to corporal, but it hardly assuaged my grief over losing the chance of seeing Cecilia and enjoying the unforgettable dances with her in Carnahan Hall.

Moreover, I loathed leaving Huachuca, my best army post ever. It was a small, picturesque camp, nestled in the foothills of southern Arizona's Huachuca (thunder) mountains, self-contained and well provisioned, having year-round mild weather, abundant sunshine, fresh air, and sweet water. The Twenty-fifth was the only unit there, except for a small detachment of Indian scouts in direct support of the regiment. White civilians worked and lived in close proximity to soldier's families, but not on an integrated basis. Of course, white officers lived in segregated quarters on officers' row, with their exclusive club. Yet, these officers rated among the best that I encountered in all my service.

Sizeable towns closer to the garrison were Nogales and Naco astride the United States (Arizona) and Mexico (Sonora) border. People on the Mexican side offered soldiers complete racial integration in every respect. Whites on the U.S. side, too, were friendly and respectful. They had not forgotten the protection and security the Twenty-fifth had provided them from bandits and hostile Indians during the Buffalo Soldier days. Then, too, their community businesses were nurtured with Huachuca's payroll. There were very few segregated or off-limits public places. Such "ideal" living conditions at my first army post deluded me into expecting similar qualities of soldier life at Camp Wolters.

The contrary was true. Camp Wolters/Mineral Wells mirrored the aura of Palestine, racially segregated and highly prejudiced. The camp had ten white and two black training battalions under a single colonel commander, but utilizing separate facilities and training areas. The two black units were confined to a "Colored area." The only common plant on post was the station hospital, and it had a separate ward for Negroes. I learned that this racial arrangement was typical of most military installations in America. I have also discovered that all cities and towns in our country, and in many foreign countries as well, have their black ghettos to this day. I had naively imagined otherwise, especially regarding northern and western parts of the U.S.

51

With promotion to corporal, I led the First Squad, Fourth Platoon of Company C, Sixty-sixth Training Battalion. On September 9, I graduated top student from the black NCO school and signed on to temporary military police duty (a new program at Wolters), patrolling the Colored part of Mineral Wells. Temporary MPs, untrained in police matters, were chosen by battalion commanders from among their best junior NCOs, simply to help soldiers act in an orderly manner while on pass in Mineral Wells. They were unarmed, carrying only night sticks and wearing "MP" arm bands on the left sleeve of their outer garment. Post headquarters had a company of white MPs armed with pistols and night sticks, performing regular MP duties, e.g., traffic control, manning gates to the garrison, etc.

I was first to lead a black MP patrol to Mineral Wells. As we approached the main gate to town in a 3/4 ton truck, white MPs promptly arrested us, shouting, "There's no such thing as a nigger MP!" Before I could explain, a reinforcement, led by a white MP sergeant, wrestled away our night sticks and hauled us off to post headquarters for confinement. When the duty officer saw the formation, he released us, half-heartedly reprimanding the sergeant. I got no apology. The lieutenant tried to offer regrets, explaining that the white MPs were never informed of Wolters black battalions' implementation of the new temporary MP program, nor of my mission. His chimerical attempt to reason away the debacle failed to hide both his and the white MPs' mockery of me and the concept of black MPs. I forgave them and continued my mission.

Notwithstanding, the idea and need for black MPs, even at racially diverse installations, had taken root. Wolters' white MPs and the duty lieutenant had never seen or heard of the excellent job that black MPs were doing at Huachuca. I got relieved from MP duty six weeks later, when my name came out on the promotion list to sergeant.

When the Japanese attacked Pearl Harbor, I became the Fourth Platoon leader of Company C, gaining promotion to sergeant. Chronic shortage of commissioned officers, who normally lead platoons, forced my unit to use NCOs to fill these positions.

Another first for the army and me happened in June 1942,

when Brigadier General Benjamin O. Davis, Sr. inspected Camp Wolters. Davis was the first black general in U.S. Army history and was the army's assistant inspector general. His ten-day mission was to assess the quality of training and treatment that black soldiers were receiving at the camp.

Pentagon staff generals are not assigned officer *aides de camp,* as are those in the field with troops; so, as a courtesy gesture, the post commander selected me to serve as Davis's aide during his visit. I got a "quickie" training course from the battalion adjutant on the duties of an aide to a general on an inspection visit. They were: to escort the general on inspections, take notes of comments made and conditions found; then formalize the notes with the general at supper in a special, hastily fabricated room in the battalion headquarters company mess hall, where the general took meals and had his office. Davis slept in a room at the Colored area guest house. (Even black generals could not dine or sleep in white facilities on or off post.) Detailed plans for the following day's inspections also got the general's approval.

When he returned to Washington, Davis sent copies of his detailed report to commanders at Wolters. The report concluded: "Much of the black soldiers' problems at Wolters could be traced to the prejudiced attitudes of white soldiers and to poor leadership on the part of white officers commanding black units."

Near the end of Davis's inspection, he urged me to apply for Officer Candidate School (OCS) to become a commissioned officer. I was already aware of the OCS program and had had the opportunity to apply since January. I also knew the fate of many promising NCOs who rushed into commissioned officer status during the First World War, only to realize reduction to their highest enlisted rank after Armistice Day, forfeiting the chances of rising to higher NCO grades, which were more easily held after the conflict. I shuddered at the thought of returning to buck sergeant. Davis, however, assured me that this would not happen under newly adopted procedures for OCS graduates to qualify for regular status. I then applied for OCS and was sent to the Infantry Officer Candidate School at Fort Benning, Columbus, Georgia—assignment: OC Class 164, Third Infantry Regiment.

I joined a detail of eleven white corporals selected with me to attend the same class of officer hopefuls. As a ten-month-old sergeant, I naturally assumed I would be in charge of the travel group. Not so! The senior white corporal, John Krouse, was put in charge; thus, I had to play subordinate to him throughout the trip. We traveled by truck from Wolters to Weatherford, Texas, situated on the main east-west Southern Pacific Railway track to Columbus, Georgia. (Blacks could never be in charge of whites in the segregated army.)

Arriving in Weatherford at high noon, we loaded our luggage on a Pullman train car coupled to a passenger express departing at 2:00 P.M. Using meal tickets issued for the trip, Krouse marched us across the tracks to a white restaurant for lunch. Born and raised in Omaha, Nebraska, Krouse was accustomed to whites and blacks eating together in cafés; so he seated us at a table for twelve in the main dining room. When the head waiter scrutinized me, he told Krouse I had to get lunch through the kitchen back door and eat under a tree behind the restaurant. Used to these eating arrangements for Coloreds in Palestine, I willingly complied, though my stomach was tight with indignation, for I suspected repetition of this routine would continue all the way to Benning. The army almost never moved troops by rail on luxury trains with dining cars. Indeed, our car was hitched intermittently to freight trains during the trip.

At Columbus a black jeep driver picked me up for transport to Company A's barracks, while the white candidates rode a 2-1/2 ton truck to the same location. The driver gave me some valuable advice en route, emphasizing sudden-death dangers that black candidates faced. He said: "Never go to the main post or anywhere in Columbus. White MPs, seeing that OCS patch sewn on your shirt pocket, will automatically give you a delinquency report (only one will eject you from the program) for imagined violations, e.g., out of uniform, disorderly conduct, in off-limits places, etc. whether you are guilty or not. Confine yourself to the regimental area until you graduate." I did exactly that.

Officer Candidate School compressed a regular four-year tactical and technical officer training program into ninety days. Eighteen-hour class days were common. Spot quizzes either began or ended every class, and stiffly graded tests, given at the end of every course, played a major role in determining graduation and class standing.

The toughest physical challenge was a weekly running of the obstacle course, which candidates likened to a "dash through hell." It was a half-mile labyrinth of tangled barbwire, deep trenches, wall obstacles, dried and flowing rocky stream beds. Requirement: Complete the course satisfactorily in seven minutes.

Negotiating the eight-foot wooden wall presented the hardest problem. Failure to climb over that obstacle in time washed out eighteen physically inept candidates the first week. A large pine tree stand edging the regimental compound was the arena for command voice development. Students unaccustomed to giving loud, sharp commands spent many night hours under tactical officer supervision calling those trees to attention and imaginatively drilling them around in accordance with the *Close Order Drill Manual.*

Infantry weapons training included attaining familiarity, maintenance, and acceptable marksmanship skills with every weapon in the infantry arsenal from the bayonet to the 37mm anti-tank gun. I got expert ratings with the bayonet, 30 caliber carbine, M-1 rifle, 45 caliber pistol, and the 30 caliber water-cooled machine gun; while qualifying satisfactorily with the rest.

Leadership was the star course of OCS. The crowning requirement, testing students' learning and understanding of the course, was to write in three hours a composition describing the knowledge, training, personal traits, and behavioral tendencies of a "good" military officer. This is what I wrote:

A good military officer must be a leader among soldiers. Soldiers should be able to recognize him as a leader and readily give him their respect and loyalty.

Since a military officer must be a leader, his training should provide for that goal at the outset. His first subjects should be basic and general in nature, reserving specialized skills for treatment after general areas are mastered. Formally, he should be grounded in the arts and sciences sufficiently well for acceptance as a journeyman of these phenomena. Throughout this general and basic training, leadership techniques and traits should be instilled, practiced, and emphasized. Militarily, the officer should know and do his basic subjects superbly. These basic subjects extend from military courtesy and discipline through gunnery and navigation to tactics. Throughout training the officer must keep uppermost in mind the need to apply required skills in a leadership role. Situations requiring rapid analysis and decisions, followed by supervision of execution is the ideal leader training method. Frequent changes in the situation, requiring reaction and future planning should also be introduced.

A military officer's behavior and personality should parallel the pattern we customarily associate with a "gentleman." Simplified, this means that an officer should conduct himself at all times as if he were under the direct surveillance of his parents, his pastor, and his commander. Oversimplified? Perhaps, but what other quick and tangible qualities can we attach to a gentleman? "Likable but respected" is a good description to acquire for oneself. In all situations, demonstrate loyalty and sincerity of purpose, and maintain a balance of togetherness and aloofness that demands respect. The balance varies among leaders; so each individual develops and recognizes his own. But the overriding criterion should be *respect* of your led.

Good military officers are also good managers. A workable managerial trait is always to have a plan. This was one of Napoleon's traits, which led to his many successes. When analyzing a situation (and this is always), try to imagine what could go wrong; then plan accordingly. This prevents surprise and engenders confidence. Managing means controlling and directing resources to achieve a goal. Effectiveness and efficiency are the measuring rods of management Analyze, organize, deputize, supervise, and, if necessary, penalize; but get the job done in the most effective and efficient manner possible.

Have a positive attitude. This is known as a "Can Do" attitude. No mission is too difficult, no sacrifice is too great, if duty demands it. When given a mission, think positively how well it can be done. Do not harbor negative thoughts. Such an attitude will build confidence and courage as well as loyalty. A good understanding of endurance and limits instills the compassion an officer should demonstrate. This means knowing oneself and one's charges, including their strengths and weaknesses.

As already indicated, a leader should know and do his job

outstandingly well. Knowledge is the first prerequisite of leadership. Soldiers will respect and follow a knowledgeable leader; hence job knowledge and ability to perform it are basic attributes of a good military officer. I say basic because the ultimate requirement is not only to know and do job skills, but also to apply the leadership quantum in persuading others to do likewise.

Inscribed upon the Delphic Oracle is the time-honored saying, "Know thyself." This is the signal requirement for self-discipline. In order to discipline and control others, one must first master and discipline himself. This is also the basis for teaching and leading by example. A good military officer protects human life and property. Such a leader accepts the responsibility for all his unit does or fails to do. Use subordinates to aid decision making, but never abdicate your responsibility for making decisions and accepting the full measure of the results.

Loyalty and respect should govern your relationship with subordinates and superiors alike. Avoid making promises to subordinates that you do not live up to, and never speak derogatorily of your superiors in front of your subordinates. Do not become familiar with subordinates or superiors and insure that your appearance and conduct always demand respect.

The military life is rigorous and physically demanding. You must maintain better physical fitness than your men. Do not become overweight and avoid excessive eating and drinking. These appear to be trite maxims, but they are often ignored or discovered too late for meaningful application. Force yourself to keep physically fit.

The many formal methods for maintaining "unit morale," such as, keeping the led informed, hot chow, dry socks, emphasizing unit history and tradition, and encouraging competition among units, do well, yes. But also develop a strong buddy system in your unit, and the accompanying absolute "to never let your buddy down." The idea, when developed fully, will permeate unit performance both in garrison and in combat. Every man will strive hardest not to let his buddy down, and conversely will demand premium performance from his buddy.

All five behavioral traits I have described for unit leaders fully obtain in the officer's relationship with his family. He is the leader of his family also. Develop the same unit morale among family members as you do with members of your command. Family performance will then be a constant source of pride for everyone concerned. Spend as much time with your family as your military duties permit, and avoid voluntary separations, because you are sure to get your share of involuntary ones.

—George M. Shuffer, Jr.
Officer Candidate, Class 164

My class was racially integrated, except that black candidates slept in the NCO rooms of the barracks. Whites bunked in the main squad rooms. All other areas in the company were integrated, including dining and latrine facilities. Five black candidates, including myself, started OC-164; three graduated. Staff Sergeant Earnest McDougal failed for getting caught by white MPs in Columbus. He was reported delinquent for being out of uniform, a charge most unusual for McDougal, because he was always impeccably dressed, even in pajamas. Candidate James Blevins failed academically. William Smith, Charles Skinner, and I graduated among 160 of the 220 starters. I finished number five in the class, February 2, 1943, becoming a second lieutenant, infantry.

4
Commission and World War II

Dressed in a tailor-cut officer's uniform, emblazoned with shiny Sam Brown belt, golden bars and brass after graduation, I thought: *At last I am an officer and gentleman of the United States.* Outside graduation hall returning my first salute, I fantasized myself elite and privileged. But that dream bubble whim soon vanished amidst the bleak reality of black living, regardless of rank, in pre-1965 segregated America.

Traveling from Benning across Dixie to my first commissioned duty station with the Second Airbase Security Regiment at Fort Swift, Bastrop, Texas, I still had to ride in the back seat of buses, the coal cinder car of trains, eat in the kitchen (or behind its back door) of the few cafés and restaurants that would serve Negroes, and live in the Colored area on post.

At my first officers' call, I found the seating segregated. I sat with the few black lieutenants of the regiment in the back of the room, which allowed a wide aisle separating us from the main body of white officers up front. The colonel commanding opened his address with the greeting: "Gentlemen and Colored second lieutenants!" Disappointment, frustration, and disgust so crowded my mind that I heard only scattered fragments of his thirty-minute speech. I felt like the proverbial one-legged man in a rump-kicking contest. In deep anguish, I almost cried aloud, "Why did God make us like this? What did we do wrong?"

Like the disciples asking Jesus in St. John's Gospel, John 9:1–40: "Rabbi, was it his sin or the sin of his parents that caused him to be born blind?" I clung to the erroneous idea that the crosses of life (physical disability, illness, or death of an offspring, poverty, the racial accident of birth, when it handcuffs freedom and social mobility), all, are punishments from God.

Many today feel the same way. Often people say: "Why is God punishing me? What have I done wrong? Why does God allow this or that to happen?" Faithful meditation on this Scripture event made me realize that when such questions are asked, they come from the desire for logical answers to mysteries; and this shows spiritual blindness and lack of faith. Jesus came to cure spiritual blindness, as He cured the physical blindness of the man who was the subject of the disciples' query. Jesus told them: "It was no sin either of the man or his parents that caused him to be born blind. Rather, it was to let God's works show forth in him,"—an opportunity to manifest the glory, power, and compassion of God. I deduced that when misfortune or other crosses come in life, I must accept them as God's will, and pray for the faith to believe that God's glory, power, and compassion will show forth in me.

The army deactivated the airbase security regiment five days after I arrived and sent me to the 978th Airbase Security Battalion at Camp Butner, Durham, North Carolina.

Reducing the airbase security regiment to battalion size signaled that the concept of airbase security elements was phasing out. Why have combat infantry soldiers immediately protecting airbases securely situated behind friendly lines? The army deactivated all airbase security units on August 1, 1943 and sent their personnel to fill infantry divisions.

Accordingly, I moved to the all-black (except most commissioned officers) Ninety-third Infantry Division in Camp Clipper, Needles, California to lead the Third Platoon, Anti-tank Company, 368th Infantry Regiment. I had hoped for assignment to the Twenty-fifth, my original regiment, around which the Ninety-third was formed. On reflection, I could not recall any white airbase security units ever; so I surmised the army's use of black units in this role was an extension of its First World War philosophy of employing blacks in rear area security and/or stevedore work, revealing its continuing deep-seated distrust and lack of confidence in black units fighting in serious combat missions.

The Ninety-third had performed better in combat during World War I than the Ninety-second, probably because General

John J. Pershing had assigned its regiments to the French. The French trained, supplied, and fielded them as if they were their own, without regard to race. As a result, they participated in more fighting than work or guard details. In the end, three of the Ninety-third's four regiments won the *Croix de Guerre* for valor, France's highest award for a military unit. The Ninety-third's shoulder patch pictures a blue French helmet on a black background. I was proud to wear it.

Camp Clipper was in the middle of California's Mojave Desert. The "French blue helmet division" was honing its desert warfare skills to help Allied forces in North Africa finish off General Erwin Rommel's Afrika Korps. Desert warfare involves heavy use of tanks and other armored vehicles, so I naively considered my assignment to the anti-tank company a plum. On second thought, though, I remembered Rommel's juggernaut had collapsed before the end of July. The follow-on invasion of Italy by Allied troops resurrected my hopes, because armored warfare would surely dominate the battlefield there. The Ninety-third dutifully continued its concentration on desert warfare training through autumn.

Then came alert orders moving the division to the southwest Pacific jungles by January 20, 1944 for combat in the northern Solomon Islands and the Bismarck Archipelago. We became part of General Douglas MacArthur's southwest Pacific theater reserve.

When I paid off my debt to Mrs. Scott back in October 1940, I steadily sent two-thirds of my monthly pay home to Johnnie, demanding that she spend it on herself. If she so desired, she could help GM defray college expenses for my sisters and help out with mortgage payments (which sometimes she did). This monthly amount had grown to $230 by the war's close. Johnnie instead bought war bonds with the bulk of it, listing me as co-owner. In the staging area at Camp Stoneman, California, preparing for overseas shipment, she revealed her secret, citing an accumulation of $3,780 not including interest. I was shocked and upset with the news. In letter after letter, I pleaded with her to spend the money for herself. She ignored my pleas, unceasingly adding to the pile-up. When I got home from the war, I had well over

$6,000 in war bonds. I saw and believed in the value of a strong money-saving habit, which I continue to this day.

Shortly before the Ninety-third moved to Camp Stoneman, it got equipped with and trained in the use of the new 57mm anti-tank gun, with a new projectile especially designed to wipe out enemy tanks. Imagining there would be few Japanese tanks roaming through the Solomon Island jungles in early 1944, I wondered what mission the anti-tank units would receive. Our regiment landed on Benika Island, which guarded the critical shipping lanes leading to Guadalcanal and Australia. There was a threat of Japanese seals and guerrilla forces landing on vulnerable beach areas to join pockets of "left over" Nippon units, who were harassing natives and U.S. supply and ammo dumps. The anti-tank company provided round-the-clock security at critical landing beaches.

In early 1944, the army's racial policies came under heavy attack in the United States. The black press was indignant, and organizations such as the NAACP, were contending angrily that blacks had been excluded unfairly from the army's combat actions. Seeing an opening, President Roosevelt's political opponents in Congress took up the cry. A veteran of the Ninety-third Division in World War I, Republican Congressman Hamilton Fish, of New York, declared that in a war undertaken to advance freedom, the sons of 14 million black Americans should have "the same right as any other American to train, to serve, and to fight . . . in the defense of the United States." Truman Gibson, civilian aide on Negro affairs to the Secretary of War, underscored Fish's message by noting that the Republicans clearly intended to make black participation in combat an issue in the coming presidential campaign.

Meantime, General MacArthur's strategy, in his drive from Australia to the Philippines, was to bomb furiously and bypass the principal Japanese bases, and by "leap frog" tactics, to land at unexpected, and sometimes undefended, points along the route that he must clear (See map, Southwest Pacific Area). By January 1944, he had advanced in this fashion through the Solomon Island and Bismarck Archipelago chains and begun his attack along the shores of New Guinea toward the southern Philippines.

Prodded or not by criticism back home of the army's racial policies, which unfairly excluded blacks from combat actions, MacArthur started rotating the Ninety-third and white reserve and National Guard divisions, which were less well trained, from deep theater reserve to missions of closer combat relative to elite U.S. amphibious assault landing forces. The concept envisioned using first-rate units to seize and secure substantial beachheads at desired points; then withdraw to execute similar future assaults, leaving the Ninety-third, reserve and National Guard divisions to mop up bypassed pockets of resistance, thereby securing his trail.

To assure himself that his officers were ready to accomplish their new combat tasks, Major General Harry H. Johnson, Ninety-third commander, personally conducted sand table tests at each regimental command post. The test required lieutenants and captains to analyze platoon and company situations, formulate a plan of action, and issue an oral five-paragraph field order to accomplish the objective. Eight black lieutenants and three white captains had given unsatisfactory answers to the examination at the 368th CP, when Johnson called on me to recite a solution. In the fashion of my performance at OCS (the problem in fact was very similar to one I solved there), I gave the "school" solution. Johnson was so pleased with my recitation that he ordered Colonel J. R. Urquhart, CO, 368th: "Promote this man to captain immediately!"

"He is still a second lieutenant, sir," responded Urquhart. I had polished my gold bars so well and often that they looked like silver first lieutenant insignia.

"Then make him a first lieutenant, now!" ordered Johnson.

When Johnson found out that I was an anti-tank platoon leader, he told Urquhart to assign me to a unit that will make *personal* contact with the enemy. So I took leadership of the regimental intelligence and reconnaissance (I&R) platoon that day.

I had just been discharged from the collection station, where I was confined for three days, recovering from a secondary athlete's foot infection in the right leg. During this temporary break

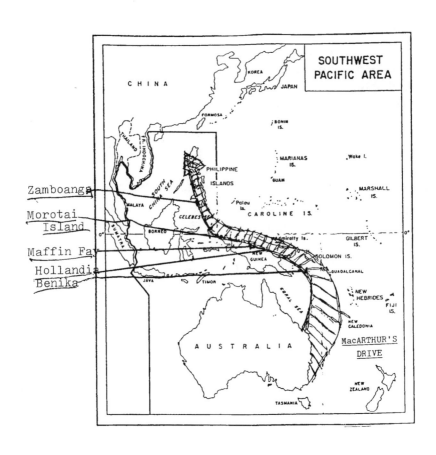

Zamboanga

Morotai
Island

Maffin Fa...

Hollandia
Benika

SOUTHWEST
PACIFIC AREA

CHINA

KOREA

JAPAN

FORMOSA

BONIN
IS.

MARIANAS
IS.

Wake I.

GUAM

MARSHALL
IS.

THAILAND

FR. INDOCHINA

PHILIPPINE

ISLANDS

Palau
Is.

CAROLINE IS.

MALAYA

SOUTH CHINA SEA

CELEBES

BORNEO

Admiralty Is.

GILBERT
IS.

0°

SUMATRA

0°

NEW
GUINEA

SOLOMON IS.

GUADALCANAL

JAVA

TIMOR

CORAL SEA

NEW
HEBRIDES

FIJI
IS.

NEW
CALEDONIA

AUSTRALIA

MacARTHUR'S
DRIVE

NEW
ZEALAND

TASMANIA

from jungle duty, I intensified correspondence with Cecilia, who was finishing senior year at Huachuca High. Her rapid responses greatly dispelled the loneliness on security watch, while deepening my love for her.

I immediately went into "real" combat with the I&R platoon, leading doughboy elements against Japanese units in the Hollandia and Maffin Bay areas of New Guinea and on Morotai Island. In April 1945, I engaged the enemy in the southern Philippines (Zamboanga Peninsula), where I killed or captured numerous Japanese "stay behind" soldiers who were terrorizing the populace. The Ninety-third commander decorated me with the Bronze Star Medal and the Combat Infantryman Badge for valorous and meritorious combat achievement. Near the war's end, I became regimental intelligence officer (S-2) and assisted in the interrogation, processing, and repatriation of over eight thousand prisoners of war.

Conflict with the Japanese virtually ended in the southwest Pacific when atomic bombs were dropped on Hiroshima and Nagasaki in August. I got rapid return privileges to the States, because I had over 100 points, qualifying me for early army release. Points were figured on length of time in service, length of time in combat, and combat decorations.

En route to my separation station at Fort Sam Houston, San Antonio, Texas, I took a ten-day delay in route at Huachuca to visit Cecilia. It was like a one-step exit/entry from hell into paradise. Cecilia, if at all possible, was more radiant, beautiful, and exciting than ever. Moreover, with Cecilia age nineteen and a high school graduate, we could enjoy the warm togetherness on dates scarcely imaginable in the Carnahan Hall dance era. Those ten days passed seemingly in a flash. Cecilia was preparing for her return to the University of Arizona at Tucson, where she would begin her sophomore year in September. I proposed marriage to take place during the coming Christmas holiday leave break between semesters. She accepted.

When I finally got to Fort Sam in late September, I immediately applied for a regular army (RA) commission. The personnel officer put me in a holding detachment while I took the physical and written examinations to compete for regular status. Meantime, I accepted a three-year extension on duty as a First Lieutenant, Army of the U.S. (AUS).

The threat of Soviet Communist expansion, and the power vacuum created by the Axis powers' defeat in the war mandated a stationary U.S. military presence in most of the areas where the war was fought. The army relied on the draft to maintain adequate personnel strengths even in a time of peace. Personnel officers pushed for retention of combat experienced officers and men, offering one, two, and three year service extension categories to fill manpower needs. I remained at Fort Sam Houston until December when I took the standard forty-five day TDY delay en route to my assignment: Company D, First Training Regiment at Fort McClellan, Anniston, Alabama, reporting not later than February 13, 1946.

I finally got home to Palestine the week before Christmas. Johnnie and GM rejoiced to see me safe and healthy, while offering prayers of thanksgiving for my return. It was the day after Christmas when I divulged my decision to stay in the army and return to Huachuca shortly after New Year's Day. GM strongly urged me to pursue a civilian career, citing his well-pronounced distaste of the army; this time, though, without anger, threats, or promises opposing my decision. I wrestled with the idea of a civilian career, but my love of military life, after five years of service, easily won out. I could not envision a civilian career, even after a college education, netting me a better endeavor than an army infantry career as an officer, forming and leading men in defense of their country. Johnnie winked her unqualified approval and support.

Cecilia was home in Huachuca for the holidays until January 16, when she would return to college. But she was pregnant with Gloria from our rapturous dates during my safari though Huachuca back in August. I was elated. I followed the same travel scheme that I used running away from home in 1940. Only this time I caught the Trailways bus at the main station downtown. Arriving at Cecilia's January 5, I also greeted Sergeant Mann, who had returned home from the war in Europe. Cecilia and I kept our marriage date (January 8, 1946) at the Pima

County courthouse in Tucson before a justice of the peace and returned to a joyous reception in Huachuca.

First Sergeant Mann, during the holidays, got orders to Fort Bliss, El Paso, Texas, to undergo his retirement physical and processing (he used the facilities at nearby William Beaumont General Hospital to complete his physical). He was ending a satisfying thirty-year career in the infantry. He and Maria were pleased to have Cecilia and me "baby sit" David and Mario and his quarters while they were in Bliss. We, nevertheless, enjoyed a glorious honeymoon at Huachuca. Cecilia planned to stay with her parents until I could find suitable quarters near McClellan, whereupon she would join me. When Mann retired in February, he moved his family to 1641 East 123rd Street in Los Angeles.

In the intervening time, I was on duty at McClellan. I got excellent grades on my RA commission tests, but the army sent me the standard "green" letter saying: "You are highly eligible but not selected at this time. You will remain under active consideration for regular status." I found out later from my friend Captain Tommy Martin in personnel at the Pentagon that my lack of college experience caused my being prevented from receiving regular status. It would take at least the equivalent of two years of college. One really needs a four-year college degree to be assured of regular promotion in any commissioned category. The army would not assign me to full-time civil schooling (though I applied numerous times); so I took college correspondence courses from the U.S. Armed Forces Institute (USAFI), an affiliate of the University of Wisconsin.

Mary Gloria, our first born, came May 3, 1946 in Las Companas Hospital, Compton, California. She received baptism on June 16 in the same church (St. Patrick's Catholic Church, 1046 East Thirty-fourth Street, Los Angeles) her mother had twenty years before.

I rented a room with kitchen and bath privileges from Mr. and Mrs. Williams on Taylor Street in Birmingham, Alabama. Family quarters were not available for black officers, because all family housing at McClellan was situated outside the Colored area where blacks were not welcome. Commuting distance from

Sister Mary Gloria Shuffer, 1972.

McClellan to Birmingham was fifty miles. Cost of rented room: $20 per month.

I took leave in June to escort Cecilia and Gloria to Birmingham, traveling by commercial aircraft. I learned that Negroes were confined to the first row of seats facing the bulkhead separating the cockpit from the passenger cabin, if the plane either took off or landed in Dixie. Returning with my family from Los Angeles to Birmingham, we landed for breakfast in Dallas. Full meals were not served on passenger aircraft in 1946. We were seated at the rail of a dilapidated food-warming case in the kitchen of the terminal restaurant, a sharply demeaning experience for Cecilia, who was living through her first incidents of segregation. A month later, we found a nice room for $20 per month in Anniston just outside of Fort McClellan. We moved to that room. Landlords: Mr. and Mrs. Hudson.

The army received a draft quota increase in summer 1946 to fill mounting vacancies caused by early discharges and retirements of older war veterans. More training cadres and additional training areas rose in need priority to ready conscripts for service in regular outfits.

In October, I took command of Company F of the Fifth Regiment (a skilled training cadre) and transferred with the unit to Fort Bragg, Fayetteville, North Carolina. Cecilia and Gloria accompanied me and lived with Mr. and Mrs. Mitchell, who rented them a room in Fayetteville. After only three weeks, we moved with the cadre to Fort Jackson, Columbia, South Carolina, where we rented a room from Mr. and Mrs. Adams at 2326 Laurel Street. All these rented rooms came with kitchen and bath free and were located in "black" town of the cities.

I became operations and training staff officer (S-3) of the Second Battalion. In November the CO elevated me to battalion executive officer, without promotion, but I held the position three months; then reverted to S-3. Record of these moves helped in evaluations down the line.

For recreation after duty hours, we went to movies, either to the theater in our area on post with no segregated seating, or to a movie house within walking distance of our rented room, where we sat in the balcony. Not to worry about baby-sitters while at movies or in church, for Cecilia carried Gloria in her arms wherever she went. I did the carrying when I accompanied her. This is to emphasize our unyielding policy of staying together as a family whenever possible.

We seldom went to the black officers' club, which was a branch of the white main club where blacks were excluded. A branch library served our area, but we had access to all materials held by the main library through an efficient library loan program. Blacks had their own gymnasium, softball and tennis courts, and chapel.

We bought our first automobile, a 1942 Saratoga Chrysler for $1,300.00 cash on February 1, 1947. A month later we transferred to Fort Dix, Wrightstown, New Jersey. I remained Bn. S-3, and traveled by car with the family from Jackson to Dix. Renting a room from Mr. and Mrs. Hudson on Main Street, Bordentown, for $25 a month, I commuted six miles to Dix. I found that Bordentown segregated blacks in higher public school grades (elementary grades were integrated), civic clubs, and residential living areas. The racial situation at Dix was identical with Fort Jackson.

My assignment at Dix lasted three and a half years, the longest term at one camp in ten years of service. We rented the room in Bordentown for two months, then moved into a two-bedroom farm house, owned by the Grangers of Urban League fame. The house had a fireplace and wall-to-wall carpeting, located at Box 5, U.S. Highway 1, Fieldsboro, New Jersey. Rent: $50 per month. It was the best, most comfortable place that we ever rented. Unhappily, the owners had to move back into their home four months later; so we moved to a small room in Mr. and Mrs. Williams' home in Roebling, New Jersey, ten miles from Dix, the worst place we ever rented.

Situated on the eastern end of the rust belt, Roebling was a factory town with a steel mill, which produced air pollution heavy with smoke and burning coal odors. This, coupled with record heat during summer 1947, clearly registered Roebling at the lowest point on "the place to live" scale.

By mid-November, Cecilia was fast approaching full term in her pregnancy with David. Luckily, I got quarters on post (Building T31-101), a single house with one bedroom, small kitchen, a living room, and bath. It was formerly the office of the colonel who commanded the 365th Infantry in the Range Road (Colored area) of Dix. David was born on the day we moved into quarters, November 21, in the army hospital on post. He received baptism on January 21, 1951 in Sacred Heart Catholic Church, Compton, California.

On July 6, 1948, I qualified for quarters T-55-19D, a newly converted troop barracks with three bedrooms, living room, dining nook, and bath with shower and tub. This was a timely upgrade, because Cecilia was pregnant with George III. We needed larger quarters.

Nineteen forty-eight was fruitful in other ways. I passed the two-year college-level equivalency GED test. This achievement along with completion of ten USAFI college courses (I made all As in every course) made me eligible to enter the Regular Army Officer Competitive Tour Program. This highly emulous design was an army-wide endeavor, in which only 20 of 600 selected company-grade officers in the program that year got RA commissions. I was selected for the tour on January 9, 1948. The cycle entailed commanding a rifle (or other) company for four months in three different battalions in the tour year. The selected's performance rating together with the battalion and regimental commanders' recommendations at the end of each four-month period were then sent to a Pentagon board for choosing the winners.

On April 5, 1949, I won. I was nominated by the President and confirmed by the Senate for appointment in the regular army in the grade of Second Lieutenant with date of rank January, 1948. Breathing a prayer of thanksgiving, I warmly remembered General Davis's promise back in 1942 and forgot my fears of returning to buck sergeant.

The good news of my victory came right after George III came to birth in Dix's station hospital on March 15. He got baptized January 21, 1951 in Sacred Heart Catholic Church, Compton, California.

Still another blessing came in 1948. President Harry S. Truman issued Executive Order 9981 on July 26, stipulating equal treatment and opportunity for all within the armed services

Captain David K. Shuffer, USAF, 1974.

George M. Shuffer III, US Navy Midshipman, Annapolis, 1969.

without regard to race, thus ending racial segregation in the military. The directive, however, allowed the military *enough* (my emphasis) time to make the change without damaging efficiency and morale. As a result, the army delayed execution of the policy for some units as late as 1958. [The Twenty-fourth Infantry, for example, went into combat in Korea in July 1950 with all-black enlisted men and mostly white officers. The regiment was finally integrated and redesignated the Fourteenth Infantry Regiment in September 1951. The army, nevertheless, was cautiously including blacks in formerly all-white units individually and with black units battalion size and smaller. The Second Infantry Division's Ninth Regiment, for example, had a black battalion integrated with commander and key officers white. When I took command of Company F, Twenty-fourth Infantry Regiment, two of my platoon leaders were white.]

I became Assistant S-3 of the 365th Regiment on August 18. I was first to integrate the all-white Ninth Infantry Division headquarters at Dix on January 15, 1950, with an assignment to G-3 Section. G-3 gave me authority to inspect company-level training in the two white training regiments as well as in the black 365th. I reported inspection findings directly to G-3, who forwarded them to unit commanders through the division commander. Everyone soon learned how thorough my inspections were and responded positively to my recommendations.

At G-3's first cocktail buffet for his officers and their ladies, which Cecilia and I attended, our reception during the first thirty minutes was cold to lukewarm. The cocktails finally broke the ice, and friendly greetings and conversation followed. Subsequently, we experienced no social problem on the job or at later social functions. In fact, each following day brought greater understanding and respect.

Cecilia at integration into the "regular" Army
and into the "white" Army, April 1949.

1st Lt. George M. Shuffer, Jr. at integration into the "regular" Army and into the "white" Army, April 1949.

5
Korean War and Recovery

The unexpected invasion of South Korea by North Korean troops alerted all units at Fort Dix. Stepped-up combat readiness action was highly visible throughout the post. On September 14, 1950, I got short notice orders to report to the Korean war zone ready for combat no later than September 30. In those sixteen fleeting days, I had to settle my family in a civilian location, move on to the CONUS departure point, fly to Japan, and use surface transportation to the Twenty-fourth Infantry Regiment, Twenty-fifth Infantry Division, which was five miles south of Seoul.

We bought and moved into 12429 Anzac Avenue, Los Angeles, which was only eight blocks from Cecilia's parents' home on 123rd Street. I thanked God for my practicing an unswerving money savings policy since my enlistment, because I had ready resources to meet this emergency. The house cost $8,500. We had no furniture (all the rooms and military quarters we occupied before were basically furnished); so we furnished the two-bedroom, one bath home, completely from Sears Roebuck for one thousand two hundred dollars. Cecilia was pregnant with Marlene before I left for Korea.

On the way, I memorized the Ninety-first Psalm, which Maria and Cecilia gave me to pray every day while I was in the war zone. The idea of praying this Psalm originated with First Sergeant Mann, who called it the "infantryman's Psalm." I reported in time and went to the Weapons Platoon, Company G, Second Battalion. Three days later we joined the Eighth Army's offensive north to the Yalu River in hopes of being home for Christmas. Morale was high.

We encountered minimal resistance in our advance. General MacArthur's invasion at Inchon, on September 15, sur-

77

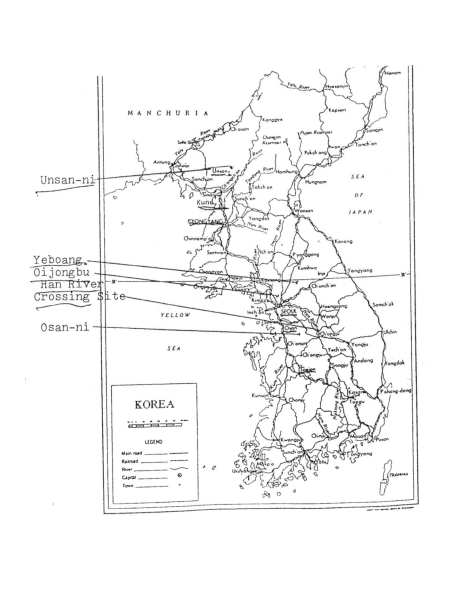

KOREA

LEGEND

Main road _____ ____
Railroad _____ ____
River _____
Capital _____ ⊙
Town _____ •

Unsan-ni
Kunu

Yeboang
Oijongbu
Han River
Crossing Site

Osan-ni

prised the North Koreans and threw their army into disarray. The Allied march turned into a "long run to the Yalu," with attacking units widely scattered, often out of communication, and their supply trains struggling to keep up.

I became executive officer of Company G later in October and moved with every attack. We dug in on Thanksgiving Day (November 23) on a high, rugged mountain fifteen hundred meters southeast of Unsan-ni. Operating on the east flank of the Twenty-fifth Division, we had orders to defend the position and maintain contact with the all-black Third Battalion of the Ninth Regiment, Second Division, on the right. (This was an experimental Negro unit, having mostly white officers, integrated with the all-white Ninth regiment.) We were prepared to continue our drive to the Yalu on order. Contact with the Third Battalion was kept through tenuous radio communication. Overly wide intervals, even between platoons, compounded by the craggy terrain, made radio contact difficult and tie-in on the ground impossible.

High-level intelligence messages revealed that large Chinese Communist forces had moved south of the Yalu to stop the Allied advance. In fact, our divisional reconnaissance troops had captured several Chinese soldiers who seemed part of enemy scouting units.

An eerie calm spread along the battlefront on Thanksgiving afternoon. Front-line company kitchens made herculean efforts to serve a hot, traditional meal to their troops that night, but failed miserably. Temperature during darkness dropped to minus 15 degrees Fahrenheit, and the steep rocky mountain slopes made their task hopeless. Food containers were frozen solid before they reached the mountain's base. Any attempt to reheat the meal would foolishly expose our positions to the enemy already poised to strike, so we ate C rations that night and dreamed of getting the nuts and raisins in number 10 cans the next day.

Harassing and interdictory artillery and mortar fires suppressed enemy movement, but our extraordinarily wide front greatly reduced their effect. Inclement weather grounded tactical air support. Shivering in our foxholes, awaiting orders to continue our attack, we gathered as much ammunition, especially hand grenades, as we could coax the Korean porters to ferry up the mountain. We had most of our winter gear; we still lacked parkas and thermal boots. Substituting woolen liners in our raincoats (intermittent snow flurries were falling) and rubber overshoes pulled over our combat boots, proved a workable solution. Our unit suffered few frostbite casualties.

Orders to continue our attack never came. Instead, at 2100 hours, the Chinese struck with a massive frontal assault, rolling us back. Reeling as we withdrew, G Company was split into two elements; I led the eastern group (approximately two platoons) southeasterly toward the Third Battalion of the Ninth's sector, and the company commander led the western element in a southwesterly direction. I made contact with the Third Battalion doughboys, who were reinforced with a tank platoon and fighting on milder grounds. We carried our wounded with us to the Third's aid station. (See sketch "Chinese Attacks, 24–25 November 1950.)

For three intense days, we fought with the Ninth Regiment, delaying the Communist drive. My men, greatly outnumbered and forced back, inflicted heavy casualties on the enemy and slowed his advance. Our efforts purchased enough time for reserve elements of the Twenty-fifth and Second Divisions to establish a defense line, which halted, albeit temporarily, the enemy onslaught. The blocking line ran east-west through Kunu-ri, a hub village in a deep valley that channeled north-south movement between Unsan and Pyong-yang. This defense forged a veritable "gap" at Kunu-ri for trapped U.S. units, now low in troop strength and with scant ammunition and supplies, to funnel south into friendly areas.

When my group passed through the gap, we rejoined Company G and the Twenty-fourth Regiment. I received the Silver Star Medal and my second award of the Combat Infantryman Badge for gallant and valorous performance. These tokens of honor, however, did not mitigate either my or the Twenty-fourth's dashed hopes of being home for Christmas, neither did it ease our painful loss of aggressive momentum to the shocking Chinese drive. Morale was low.

The following two months (until January 30, 1951), all

Chinese Attacks 24/25 November 1950

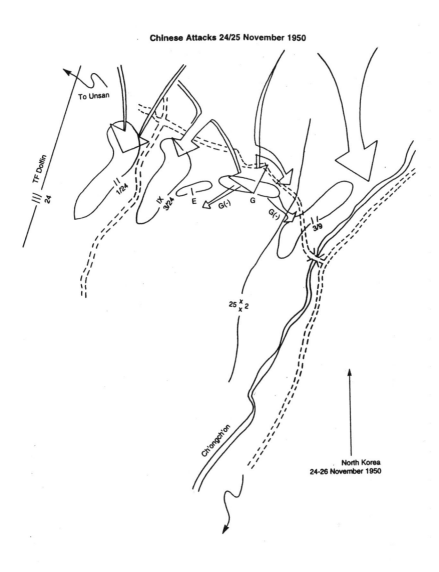

To Unsan

TF Dolfin

24

||
1/24

IX

3/24

E

G(-)

G

G(-)

||
3/9

25 ×2

Ch'ongch'on

North Korea
24-26 November 1950

Eighth Army forces fought delaying actions and withdrew south through Seoul across the Han River to Osan-ni. General Walton H. Walker was killed in a jeep accident, and offense-minded General Matthew B. Ridgeway took command, ordering "no more withdrawals, only attacks!" His army came to full strength with fresh replacements, and received the new 3.5 Rocket Launcher (able to kill any tank and "bust" any bunker), improved medium tanks, and heavier artillery. The army also now had shorter and better supply routes.

On February 2, 1951, the Eighth began its counteroffensive north. I took command of Company F and moved with the attack.

Planning got under way for an assault crossing of the Han River east of Seoul. The South Korean Army received the sector and mission to seize Seoul. My company got the prize to spearhead the western site of the Eighth Army's river assault. (See Han River Crossing sketch.)

At 0600 hours on March 7, the attack began. Using twenty-man assault boats, the fire support of six sorties of tactical aircraft, and eleven artillery battalions, my company crossed the river in three waves with ease and seized its objective, a rough mountain stronghold, which dominated river crossing points chosen for other friendly units to use. The twenty-minute preparatory bombardment was so furious and effective that it left Chinese defenders at the river's edge drunk with concussion. We captured over a hundred groggy prisoners in the first ten minutes out of the assault boats. During our ascent of the mountain to our objective, we killed 153 enemy soldiers, who fiercely resisted our advance.

Company F suffered nine killed and twenty-eight wounded. By nightfall, all other elements of the Second Battalion crossed the river safely and dug in adjacent to my charges. [Some after-action reports and write-ups say: "Strong river currents and waves confused our crossing and delayed our seizure of the objective."] This is not correct. My company's three waves had finished crossing the river without any difficulty or delay. After sun-up, high waves and strong currents did develop, but they affected reserve and support troops, and the engineers, who constructed a pontoon bridge at the site.

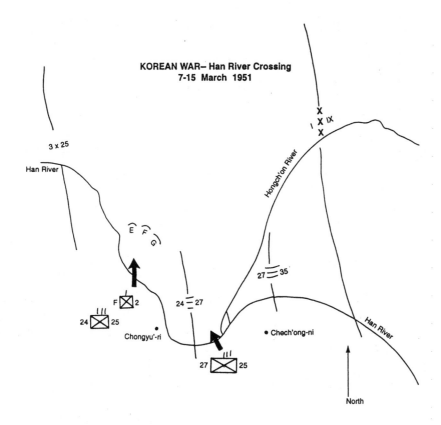

KOREAN WAR– Han River Crossing
7-15 March 1951

At 2000 hours, the enemy counterattacked, overrunning a squad of my forward platoon, which fell back to the command post. There we stopped them with massive artillery barrages and close-range grenade and small arms fire. We fought all that night, the next day, and into darkness on March 8th. The Chinese gave up and withdrew that night, and I continued the attack on March 9th, following Company K, which passed through my unit at 0600 hours. For this battle victory, I received a second Silver Star Medal (I was recommended for the Distinguished Service Cross, but higher-ups, I was told, dropped it to the silver Star) for gallantry in action.

Continuing the attack on April 16, I crossed the Hant' an River and struck an enemy mountain fastness in the POGAE SAN range near Yeboang. Heavy Communist resistance prevented me from reaching the mountaintop before dark. I dug in three hundred meters from the crest, intending to take the peak the next day. Just after twilight, a lone Chinese 120mm mortar round hit my CP and weapons platoon, wounding sixteen men. I was among them, suffering a serious head wound in the left jaw, neck, and side below the rib cage. The bent helmet, blown from my head, deflected a larger fragment aimed at penetrating my skull. A smaller piece passed between the common carotid and jugular, injuring both but severing neither, stopping close to my neck vertebrae. Thank God I recited the Ninety-first Psalm three times that day! A larger missile shattered my left mandible; smaller ones went into my left torso above the pelvis. (See sketch "Attack in the POGAE SAN area.")

It was after midnight before I reached the aid station at the foot of the mountain. Second Lieutenant Thaddeus Maladowciez, my artillery forward observer, brought me down the mountain, draped over his shoulder. He is white and six feet, five inches tall, and a former fullback for the University of Oklahoma. The other wounded were only slightly hurt and got patched up on the mountain to continue fighting.

After stabilization at the Forty-third MASH at Oijongbu, I began a long, arduous medical evacuation, passing through South Korea, Japan, Guam, Midway, Hawaii, California, Colorado, and Texas to Walter Reed General Hospital in Washing-

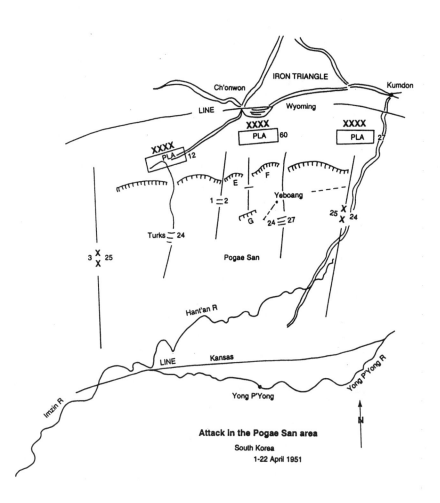

Attack in the Pogae San area

South Korea

1-22 April 1951

ton, D.C., arriving on May 12. Along the way I underwent two surgeries.

I remained hospitalized at Walter Reed fifteen months before restoration to duty. The army promoted me to captain on June 26 and decorated me with my second Bronze Star Medal and the Purple Heart Medal for battle excellence at Yeboang. Between five major operations to repair my wounds, I took thirty to forty day sick leaves for rest and recuperation at home in Compton; that is, after each operation and a short recovery period in the hospital. I would travel cross-country home on leave; then return for the next operation.

On the first leave, I greeted Marlene, our newborn, who came on June 13, in Harbor General Hospital, Torrence, California. Cecilia was unable to get to Camp Pendleton, the nearest military hospital to Compton (in those days there was no Champus program, and the army would not reimburse hospitalization costs incurred in civilian medical care facilities). Marlene received baptism on November 11, in the same church that her mother and Gloria had earlier.

With Marlene came the realization that my home on Anzac would soon be inadequate for my growing family; so I repaired and painted it for sale. A kindly visitor came one day in August and offered to buy it for $10,000. I sold it to him for closing on September 15. We bought a new three-bedroom house at 1209 West Piru Street in Compton, and delayed occupancy until October 1, to coincide the transition with my next sick leave. New house cost: $10,500.

My roommate in Ward 9A at Walter Reed was Captain Fred Stankowski, a physician and radiologist, who was accidentally hit by a speeding pickup in Columbia, South Carolina. He was recovering from multiple fractures and lacerations. He was also a devout Catholic and able Bible scholar, which I thought unusual for an army doctor. Fred and I often discussed Bible stories and passages as I attempted to smoke (smoking in bed was permitted in army hospitals then). I had started smoking cigarettes at age fifteen while in high school. By the time I got to Walter Reed at age twenty-seven, I had become a three-pack-a-day lover

86

Marlene E. Shuffer, 1969.

of Camels. I began to notice Fred's discomfiture every time I lit up and would immediately snuff out the cigarette.

Ward 9A was a combined cancer and orthopaedic surgery section where Fred and I watched expired patients taken from the ward daily. One day Fred told me: "You better quit smoking now, because your likelihood of dying from cancer grows higher with every puff." He added: "You will rarely see a radiologist smoking, because they know the score. Practically every expired person you see taken from this ward is a cancer death from smoking."

Shocked at his blunt statement, I promised to quit, though thoughts of getting a second opinion crossed my mind. Johnnie and Cecilia had often begged me to quit, but I truly loved smoking; I was totally hooked, it was locked into my senses and psyche. Then, I began wondering if I really could quit. *All things are possible through Christ who strengthens me*, I remembered reading somewhere in the Bible; so I made a New Year's resolution to quit cold turkey. After a series of stopping and restarting, I finally broke the habit on May 12th (Mother's Day), 1952.

Then I began tasting food again, and it tasted good, so good, in fact, I gained twelve pounds in three months. In a mild panic, I quit eating all sweets and saturated fats. Without cigarettes, I felt more alert and energetic, but lazy from inactivity, spending too much time in bed or sitting at Walter Reed. My first operation repaired the carotid and jugular fistula from my neck wound and allowed me to resume full physical activity. I started swimming laps in the indoor pool, gradually increasing the amount daily. Before long, I lost the extra pounds and regained weight control.

Intense study of the Bible, with Fred's help, occupied my mind. I noticed he used a different Bible during our study. He had the Douay-Rheims English translation of the Bible from the Vulgate, for Roman Catholics, while I had the King James Version used by Protestants. I thought all Christian churches used the same Bible, and all Bibles were the same. Not so! The Catholic version has seven more books than the King James Version, all in the Old Testament. They are: (Historical Books) Tobit, Judith, First and Second Maccabees; (Wisdom Books) Wisdom and

88

Sirach; and (Prophetic Book) Baruch. During the Protestant Reformation, Martin Luther, on his own authority, dropped these books from the Catholic Canon of the Bible, ruling that they were deuterocanonical (secondary) or not truly God inspired. Luther and other scholars made additional changes in passages of Isaiah and Daniel and changed some wording in the Book of James.

The first position we agreed upon was that the Bible was not the means left by Christ for the faithful to acquire a full, definitive knowledge of His teachings and take His place as Teacher. The Bible does not teach Christ's truths clearly and explicitly, because they are clothed in a language that is often obscure and seems at times almost contradictory. St. Augustine, a keen minded, learned student of Scripture, declared, ". . . there are in the Bible more things that I do not understand than things whose meaning I grasp." Then too, one man finds in Scripture clear, convincing evidence concerning some doctrine. Another may find the same text, the same verse, just as clear and convincing to him, to make him deny this doctrine.

We found also that in no way are the teachings of Scripture complete. Nowhere do they state they contain all that Christ taught. As a matter of fact, they declare the contrary. In his Gospel's last chapter and verse, St. John says: "Many things that Jesus did were omitted." Thus the Bible cannot be the sole and sufficient rule of faith. Jesus never wrote a rule of faith, nor commanded anyone else to write. Sixty years passed after Christ's Ascension before St. John wrote his Gospel, and nearly sixteen centuries after Christ, all books, including the Bible, were so rare and costly that only a few could possess them.

Yet Christ directed that all nations must be taught until the end of time. How to bring God's teachings and commands to all future generations with certainty and authority? One thing is sure, this could not be done by a book. A book that men could mutilate, change, add new phrases and words, or take out whole pages, complete chapters and books. And by using such deception could compel Christ's words to mean what they wanted them to mean. We agreed that not to realize this was to challenge the wisdom of God Himself!

Our reasoning and intelligence told us that the only way by which Christ could have left His teachings to mankind was by the means of an organization—a living, visible, teaching organization. That was even the Jewish conception of Christ. That is why He was known as the Messiah. For the Messiah was to bring into being the new kingdom. And that is what happened. Christ proclaimed to Pilate: "He was a King!" He also pronounced to the world: "My Church is My Kingdom!"

Fred invited me to Mass at the hospital chapel (I pushed him there in a wheelchair. He was making great recovery). I was impressed by the people's devotion, genuflecting to the Real Presence (God) in the Tabernacle upon entering and leaving the church, kneeling during the Eucharistic prayer and standing for all others, and kneeling to receive Holy Communion. All females wore head coverings, even infants; and priests and altar boys radiated great piety. The liturgy, all in Latin, except for the Gospel and homily, which were in English, was strange to me.

Fred almost reasoned me into accepting that the Catholic Church is Christ's Kingdom. I needed more time and much more prayer to acquire the faith.

Still confined to Walter Reed getting my mandible rebuilt, I took a college correspondence law course from LaSalle Extension University in Chicago. LaSalle promised an LL.B. Degree after three years study. I was speeding halfway through the course before realizing that LaSalle was an unaccredited institution not recognized by the army or any accredited college. I immediately dropped the course, hoping to find an accredited place to study at my next assignment. Cecilia got pregnant with Rita in late January 1952.

6
A New Faith

Fully recovered from my wounds, I reported for duty as S-3, Special Troops, Fort Ord, Monterey, California on September 15. The next day I registered at Monterey Peninsula College Evening School in pursuit of an Associate in Arts Degree in Education. We moved into Quarters 2856D, Pacific Heights. It was another three-bedroom apartment in a converted troop barracks. I rented out my house on Piru Street in Compton.

Rita's nativity occurred in Fort Ord's hospital on October 8, 1852. She received initiation into Christianity on June 17 in the same church that her mother had. A month after Rita's birth, we moved into a four-bedroom set of quarters (2835A, Pacific Heights) across the street from 2856D.

On December 11, I took command of Headquarters Company, 6003 Army Support Unit, a company with over a thousand administrative and logistical soldiers. Just integrated under the army's new Race Integration Program, the organization offered my first racially mixed command experience. The 6003 had flunked its two previous annual Inspector General (IG) tests, and, on probation, faced a third. Consecutive unsatisfactory commanders had allowed basic army standards to deteriorate below par in practically every aspect of military life. Soldier appearance, discipline, and qualification skills had fallen below the merest expectation, even for housekeeping troops.

The company was home to personnel assigned to the post motor pool, cooks and bakers school, post finance office, headquarters staff sections, signal, ordnance, quartermaster warehouses, and salvage yard. These, despite their mundane specialties, were still expected to carry weapons and fight as infantry. [This was borne out in Korea, where I frequently used

Rita C. Shuffer, 1972.

headquarters and kitchen soldiers (cooks) to reinforce company defenses, even to join in local counterattacks.] There was no evidence of an inventory of company property in the past two years. Barracks and company areas were unkempt and maintenance neglected. Smelly latrines with toilets that belched instead of flushed, broken mirrors, and burned-out light bulbs, companioned squad rooms with sloppily made bunks and empty beer cans on the floor. Most of the men lived off post. They came directly to their work places and returned to their abodes without company officers ever seeing or knowing them. Soldiers were uniformly overweight and lacking required physical strength. Company fund books were out of balance.

Since their work place duty hours were from 0800 to 1700, five and a half days per week, I had to set an extra duty and training routine to correct their soldier skills deficiencies. I called mandatory reveille (100 percent muster) for all officers and men at 0500 hours Monday through Saturday. We conducted training and work periods until 0700 hours, when they had breakfast; then went to their work places by 0800. From 1700 to 1800, they returned to the company to participate in a rigorous physical training period and an equipment and weapons accounting and maintenance period. Those with lingering barracks and latrine cleaning and maintenance problems stayed an additional hour. Saturday afternoons were spent practicing weapons qualifications skills on the firing ranges. Additionally, we spent some evenings until 2100 hours honing night-firing techniques.

This intense training and maintenance schedule lasted a month. Afterward, as men achieved required standards, they were relieved from the schedule. Those failing to qualify, continued the program until they met expected skills. All officers and senior NCOs, including myself, took and passed every test required of the men. Moreover, all leaders and I were in the company, working closely with the men, teaching and supervising them daily, including many Sundays.

Six weeks in command, I brought the unit up to *Excellent* on the IG inspection. In the process, the Special Troops commander, LTC Roy A. Stephenson, rated me *Low Satisfactory,* declaring I was too hard on administrative-logistical type soldiers and relieved me of command "without prejudice." He recommended that I be transferred to a rifle company "where I could keep soldiers under my thumb."

Major General Robert B. McClure, Commanding General, Sixth Infantry Division and Fort Ord, disapproved the relief order and threw out the low efficiency report, but reassigned me to Division Faculty, which taught leadership and teaching skills to company-grade officers as instructors. I became Chief, General Subjects Committee. Lesson learned: When deemed too hard on lax troops, work harder with them, only stay fair and just. McClure thought I had done a marvelous job commanding the 6003rd.

I graduated from Monterey Peninsula with an AA Degree (Education) on May 28, 1953. The army selected me to attend the Infantry Officer (Career) Course at Fort Benning beginning January 1954. Before Christmas 1953, we moved to #1 Battle Park, Fort Benning, enrolling Gloria and David in post schools (racially integrated) for the 1954 spring semester.

Benning was quite different from my OCS days. All army units were integrated, and all facilities served blacks equally with whites, including the main officers' club. Downtown Columbus, though, remained rigidly segregated. Blacks, including visiting soldiers, generally confined themselves to Colored town. Patrolling white MPs were courteous to blacks, if they remained in their segregated area and were orderly.

The advanced course aimed at making "Ph.D.s" in infantry of its graduates. Students spent practically every waking hour in class or studying. Course objective was to qualify officers for command and staff duties at battalion and regimental levels. Most in my class were captains, but there also were three first lieutenants, seven majors, and three lieutenant colonels (LTCs). I graduated number 20 in a class of 175 students, and got assigned to the Second Armored Division in Germany. Reporting date: September 6.

Cecilia and the children could not travel concurrently with me to Germany, because government family quarters, still under construction, would not be ready for occupancy until January

94

1955. If I wanted my family with me before that time, I would have to select an army-approved place to rent from the Germans on their economy. So I took the family to our home on Piru Street and traveled unaccompanied, reporting for duty as S-3, Forty-third Armored Infantry Battalion. I served there until November 19, when I took the duties of S-2, intelligence officer.

I got approval for Hermann Schmidt, who spoke only German (spurring me to learn the language more quickly) to rent us three rooms, with bath and kitchen privileges in his house at #1 Einstrasse, Altenglan. Cost: 212.50 deutschmarks ($50) per month. Altenglan is ten kilometers from Baumholder; so I rented a 1940 Opel sedan until my station wagon could be shipped from the States.

Meanwhile, Cecilia and the children were proceeding cross-country in the station wagon from Compton to New York City. They arrived in a rainstorm on Halloween. She turned in the station wagon at the port over in Bayonne, New Jersey and rode a bus to her hotel in Fort Hamilton. On November 4, they flew Pan American from New York's Idlewild airport, stopping in Prestwick, Scotland, before landing at Frankfurt on November 5. Other than the children's suffering car and air sickness, they had a good trip.

I met them in Frankfurt and brought them to Altenglan where it was snowing. It was cold living with the Schmidts, who followed German tradition of keeping household temperatures no warmer than 55 degrees Fahrenheit daytime and 50 at night. Instead of blankets Germans use a *stepdecker* (a thick comforter) for bed covering. It was heavy and clumsy to use at first, but the cold nights soon made you expert at staying under it. Accustomed to balmy California, Cecilia and the children felt little comfort until they moved into new government quarters at 8818 Apartment 3A (four bedrooms), Baumholder Sub Area, on January 12, 1955.

Shortly after arrival back in September, I enrolled in the University of Maryland (Europe) Overseas Program in pursuit of a Bachelor of Science Degree in Military Science. The program conducted three-hour class sessions after duty hours four evenings (Mondays through Thursday) every week for eight weeks per semester. Each college course required two nights each week; hence the maximum load a student could take per semester was two courses. I took German I and Western Civilization I for starters, which required me to attend classes four consecutive nights per week for eight weeks to acquire six residential college credits my first semester. I kept this pace until completion of requirements for the degree in August 1956.

Luckily, my first courses were scheduled at Baumholder when I arrived. Baumholder, however, was an outpost (field training area) for transitory units taking maneuver training tests. Course scheduling was scant compared to larger, hub areas in Germany, e.g., Munich, Kaiserslautern/Ramstein, Frankfurt, Augsburg, etc., where courses were plentiful and varied. The university worked hard to accommodate students in outlying areas by rotating instructors and courses, but every student inevitably had to travel extensively to complete courses necessary for graduation. For example, in my final semester, I drove the station wagon 290 kilometers twice a week for eight weeks to complete two, hard to find, but required, courses for graduation.

The years 1954–57 witnessed continuing high cold war tensions between Soviet and NATO forces, especially in Germany. Military units on both sides lived in a semi-combat alert status, spending an average of seven months each year in the field on war maneuvers with full basic loads of ammunition and other supplies.

Military dependents kept emergency baggage packed and evacuation routes memorized to escape harm's way in case fighting broke out. This left little time for recreation and leisure.

In spite of these demanding duty requirements, I maintained progress toward my degree apace. Tightening the routine further, I graduated from the USAREUR (United States Army, Europe) Intelligence and Military Police School at Oberammergau (a required course for S-2s) May 30, 1955 as the Honor Student. When I finally got my BS Degree in August with the Class of 1956, I did so with scholastic honors. During this duty tour in Europe, my children attended U.S. military dependent schools in Baumholder which were highly accredited throughout the fifties.

During the same time, my family and I grew spiritually, as I was converted to the Catholic Church on March 30, 1957. Before, I attended Protestant chapel every Sunday after joining the army, mainly because I loved to pray and worship, and I realized spiritual value from praying and studying the Bible. My leadership experience also encouraged my desire to be seen by my men and the community "going to church." I continued the practice with my family, who were Catholic, but to keep me happy and peaceful, they quietly attended Protestant service with me.

Then one Sunday late in 1956, Gloria saw Father Ambrose E. McGuire, a Catholic Chaplain (First Lieutenant) talking with some of her friends after Mass. In Baumholder, Protestant service followed Mass in Chapel #1, and, for a few minutes, the two congregations (Catholics leaving and Protestants arriving) mingled outside the chapel while assistants changed the chapel setup from Catholic to Protestant. Recognizing her best friend talking with Father, Gloria (age ten) skipped over to the priest and blurted out: "My mother and I are Catholics, too." After recovering from the surprise, the priest requested a house call with Cecilia and me.

When he came, he persuaded me to allow Cecilia and the children to practice their faith and attend Mass, since they were obliged to do so under the pain of mortal sin. "As for you, sir," Father said, "you are not obliged to attend Mass, but you are welcome anytime."

I declined his invitation, but I did not voice objection to my family attending, feeling confident, they, after a couple of Sundays, would rush back to Protestant service, breathing a sigh of relief with every step. I remembered the strangeness that I felt in Mass at Walter Reed.

But they did not come back, and I felt so cold and lonely sitting on that church bench alone without the warm support of their presence. My attention and interest evaporated at service in the wake of thoughts and longing to be with them. Besides, I noticed they were smugly happy about going to Mass. I could not remember ever seeing them so relieved and comfortable on Sundays.

After several faith arguments with Cecilia, I agreed to visit

97

Mass with her. As we walked from the parking lot to the chapel (Chapel #2), I felt self-conscious, wishing I were invisible, because I did not want any Protestants to see me going to Mass. I did not mind going to Mass that time at Walter Reed, because I was among strangers.

Relieved, I found none of my non-Catholic friends said anything. Even the people at Mass appeared unaware of my awkwardness and confusion with Latin and times for standing, sitting, and kneeling. Catholics there were friendly and happy to see me. The most settling thing: I was in Church with my family, and they were happy. I continued attending Mass, feeling, "if you cannot whip them, join them."

Yet, I became more curious about the Church and Mass. There were many things that I did not understand, and I wanted to know, because I still felt "left out" from my family.

Father announced an inquiry class beginning after New Year's Day, and he invited me to attend. I accepted despite strong warnings from the Protestant chaplain to be wary of papal authority, former "bad" popes, confessions to a priest, and worshiping the Communion wafer as God. I was cautious, and I questioned the priest at length. But I was surprised at how little I knew about my own non-Catholic faith. I believed in God, I thought, but I did not understand *what* I believed. There was a watered-down version of the Apostle's Creed, which, in some chapels, was recited once or twice a year, but I was indifferent. I had no reasonable understanding of what it meant.

Then I came to the key Truth leading to my conversion; that is, believing Jesus, who is the Christ, is God Himself! Before, I held him as a godly person, a miracle worker, yes, even the Son of God, but someone less than the Father. I had read many times Christ's statement: "I and the Father are one" in St. John's Gospel, but I had not realized its shattering truth; namely, Jesus Christ is God Himself! He did what only God can do: Cured the sick of every ailment, gave sight to the blind, made cripples walk and lepers whole, raised the dead. The strongest proof: He raised Himself from the dead and proved He is alive. *I am the Good Shepard,* says Jesus in St. John's Gospel. *I know my sheep and my sheep know me. In the same way that the Father knows me and I know the Father . . . for these sheep, I will give my life. . . . The Father loves me for this: that I lay down my life to take it up again. No one takes it from me; I lay it down freely. I have the power to lay it down, and I have the power to take it up again. . . . This command I received from my Father. John 10:14–18.* Lastly, He said He is God. He is the Second Person of the Holy Trinity, the divine Three who are One in love.

Once I believed this critical aspect of Catholic faith, everything else fell into place. Because God who revealed these truths cannot err. He cannot deceive nor can He be deceived. Christ established His Church and made Peter its head when He said: *"Blest are you Simon son of John! . . . And I say to thee: That thou art Rock (Peter) and upon this rock, I will build my Church and the gates of hell will not prevail against it.* And I will give to thee the keys of the kingdom of heaven. And whatsoever that thou shall bind upon earth, it shall be bound also in heaven; And whatsoever thou shall loose on earth, it shall be loosed in heaven" (Mt.:16:17, 19).

Thus Christ made Peter the Rock or foundation of the Church, which all the power of hell can never push over. Christ then gave Peter the keys of the kingdom of heaven and the power to bind and loose on earth. In other words He gave Peter supreme authority in His Church. With those words Jesus made Peter the first pope. Whatever laws in the realm of religion that Peter made on earth, these would be ratified in heaven. Christ gave Peter the power of freedom from error when officially teaching the universal Church.

As the Church was to continue long after Peter had died, it was rightly understood from the beginning that the privileges given him, and that were necessary for the successful mission of the Church, were given to his lawful successors—the popes. Through the gift of infallibility, He assured us that whatever we were commanded to believe (faith) or to do (morals) would always be what He and His heavenly Father wanted us to believe and to do.

Confessing my sins to a priest was the most difficult and frightening aspect of my conversion. It was the steepest of all the hills that I had to climb. And, like most other good senses of value and measurements of magnitude in life born of tough effort, it was the most rewarding and healing.

Big reason it was tough: I had already lived thirty-three unremitted years, sixteen of which had been spent in the army infantry. This included foxhole service in two wars and many sins. I dreaded confession because I knew I had to tell the priest and Almighty God really like it was and is, and that I was genuinely sorry. I examined my conscious, and I felt profoundly guilty. I was both ashamed and afraid.

But thanks be to God, Father drilled into me the idea that, yes, God is just, but He is not guided by a human concept of justice. God is merciful, understanding, and forgiving, and priests are also. Once in the confessional, I was not ridiculed, shamed, chewed out, or lectured. I lost no human dignity in there. On the contrary, I listened to the priest's advice and heard the consoling words of absolution. I felt indescribably relieved, happy, and peaceful.

Imagine how terrible it would be if God refused to forgive us our sins, or if we could never be sure whether He did forgive us! This was the Catholic reasoning that clinched my conversion. Oh, as a non-Catholic, I used to say: "I confess all my sins directly to God." But I never really did. It just sounded good to say such a thing. It was my choice defense mechanism. Even if one does confess his sins directly to God, how can he be sure whether he has been forgiven?

What a relief it was for me to consider the words that Christ spoke to the Apostles and their successors, when He said: "Receive the Holy Spirit. If you forgive men's sins, they are forgiven them; if you hold them bound (sins, that is), they are held bound" (John 20:22–23). this is how Christ instituted the sacrament of Penance (Confession).

God expresses His magnificent mercy in this sacrament chiefly through a single word: "Absolve." Speaking through the person of the priest, Jesus Himself will declare to you: "I absolve you from your sins." To *absolve* literally means to set free, as release from an obligation. It is helpful to hear the word *absolve* said aloud. There is a certain ring to it, a ring of finality. It is related to *absolute,* which means perfect, complete, certain. When we are repentant, God does not forgive us as we may sometimes say, "I forgive you, but I just cannot forget." No, God absolves us from our sins. He completely blots out the past and gives us a whole new start.

Believing in the Real Presence of God in the Holy Eucharist (Holy Communion Bread) is an act of faith. God gives us that faith, but we must use human reason and prayer to acquire it. My instructor priest used the following story and explanation that helped me accept God's gift of faith.

"A little girl had received the present of a crucifix from her father. As the two had the crucifix before them, the father asked: 'Do you know the difference between the figure of Jesus on the cross and the Sacred Host which the priest holds up at Mass?' The girl's reply is a lesson for us.

" 'When I look at the cross,' she replied, 'I see Jesus and He is not there. When I look at the Host, I do not see Jesus and He is there!' Believing in the mystery of Christ's real presence in the sacrament of the Holy Eucharist is a sincere act of faith."

It was at the Last Supper the night before He died when Christ gave the gift of Himself to us. Toward the end of that ritualistic meal of the Jewish religion, Christ took bread, blessed it and broke it, and said, "This is my body." Then taking the chalice of wine, he spoke the words, "This is my blood." However difficult that truth may have been to understand, the Apostles saw that Christ's words could have only one meaning: He was giving His body and blood for the spiritual nourishment of the world. "This is my body. This is my blood." No language could be simpler. And if we depart from the obvious meaning of the words, it is impossible to attach any meaning to them. If those words of Christ do not mean just what they say, Christ is using sentences that are incoherent, or what is worse, deceiving us.

The little group at the Last Supper must have seen that this was the fulfillment of Christ's promise made a year before just after the miracle of the loaves when He fed over five thousand.

Moreover, Christ gave the Apostles, His first priests, the power to do what He had just done. He commanded them, "Do this as a remembrance of me." In every Mass, as the priest repeats Christ's words, "This is my body . . . This is my blood,"

Christ becomes present under the appearances of bread and wine. The Host still looks the same, tastes the same.

Of all the mysteries, this is the most staggering and stupendous. To the incredulous and head-shaking non-Catholic who protests, "This is too much; how can you accept it?" There is only one answer: We take God's word for it. "I believe in God!" we say. How can we say it and not take His word as truth? We do not claim to understand how it can be. But on God's own word, we believe it is. And we have two strong props to support our belief.

The first is that long before the Last Supper, Jesus had foretold and promised in the town of Capernaum what He would do in Jerusalem on Holy Thursday. He had solemnly declared, "The bread I will give you is my flesh for the life of the world." The reaction then was skepticism. Scripture says some of His followers muttered, "This sort of talk is had to endure! How can anyone take it seriously?" From this time on, many of His disciples broke away and would not remain in His company any longer.

So what did Christ do? Nothing. Absolutely nothing. Did He call them back and say, "Look, you misunderstand me. I was speaking poetically not literally. I really didn't mean it that way at all!" Far from it! He had spoken simply and plainly. they had understood clearly and rightly. Because He meant what He said. He had no choice but to let the unbelievers go.

The second sturdy prop under Catholic belief is this: Fountains of miracles, by which Christ proved His divine power, now began to spurt forth after His promise. He opened blind eyes and deaf ears, stilled the stormy seas, and drew the dead from their grave. There were miracles pointing in prophecy toward the Mass, as when He multiplied bread on the mountaintop, foreshadowing His presence among all the Hosts distributed in the Communion lines. And changing of water into wine at Cana subtly anticipated His power to change wine into His own blood.

It was only after this long procession of glittering miracles to establish His Almighty power that Jesus fulfilled His promise. The night before He died to redeem us, He took bread into His hands and said, "This is my body." Could it be said more clearly? Note He did not say, "This is like my body," or "This is a symbol of my body," or "This is a souvenir of my body," or "This is a memorial of my body," but simply and solely, "This is my body."

And this is how the Apostles and the early Church understood it. St. Paul asks in his letter to the Corinthians, "Is not the bread we break a sharing in the body of Christ? . . . This means that whoever eats the bread or drinks the cup of the Lord unworthily sins against the body and blood of the Lord." For fifteen hundred years, the whole Christian Church never dreamed of any other meaning. Since then not one jot or iota of scriptural evidence has ever come forward to warrant a different interpretation.

The Scriptures have not changed, but at one period of history, it seems that the hearts of men did change. When some of them began to throw over the hard, thorny elements of religion, when they found it too hard to gather around the altar for worship every Sunday, when they found it too hard to confess their sins to a priest, when they found it too hard to live with one spouse till death did they part, when they found it too hard to acknowledge the pope as the successor of Peter as visible head of the whole Church; then they found it too hard to believe in the Real Presence of God in the Holy Eucharist. And they turned away from it.

As natural food nourishes us and builds us up, giving us the needed strength to take care of our daily duties, so the Holy Eucharist accomplishes these things for us spiritually by increasing sanctifying grace in us. Without this grace, we cannot be saved.

I was converted to the Catholic faith by these compelling instructions and the grace of God. I received baptism on March 30, 1957 conditionally in case my previous baptism was invalid. I also got First Confession, First Holy Communion, and (with Cecilia) matrimony in the Church before a priest on that same day. Father McGuire presided at Chapel #1 in Baumholder. Major and Mrs. (Rita) James L. Keown served as Godparents and marriage witnesses. Major Keown was S-3, Combat Command C, Second Armored Division, and I was his assistant.

7

Career Seasoning

After conversion to the Church, I took an oft deferred and much deserved leave with the family to Rome. We visited all the holy sites, beginning with the immense basilica, St. Peter's Church. When you approach the Eternal City from any direction, you can see its massive dome miles away. It has invoked the admiration of billions independently of their religion. Rising nearly five hundred feet, it is supported upon a large rock platform in the shape of a large cross, and there is almost as much stone underneath the ground as there is above it.

Beneath the dome of this great church, one can descend by marble stairs to a little crypt. We saw some people kneeling, some even kissing the floor. Tradition has always affirmed a belief, now almost definitely confirmed by scientific data obtained from recent extensive excavations, that directly under this hallowed spot lies buried the body of St. Peter. The basilica is set on what was formerly a gigantic stadium capable of seating two hundred thousand people. One could spend a week just going through this vast church, appreciating its art and structure, not to mention the spiritual import of the Masses and benedictions.

There are many other interesting sites in Rome, but the one other equally outstanding for us was the Catacombs. Underneath the outskirts of the city, through the countryside, these underground tunnels, about twelve feet wide, have walls of solid stone. If these labrynthine caverns were put in one straight line, they would extend the astounding length of five hundred miles, and, as they have two sides, we could regard them as walls one thousand miles long.

On these walls one can see paintings, carvings, pictures, symbols as well as inscriptions in Greek and Latin, giving a résumé of the chief events of the Old Testament. These walls also display graphic evidence of the doctrines and practice of the Catholic Church. We were fortunate to attend Mass at one of many altars in the east Catacombs where early Christian martyrs worshiped in secret to escape the clutches of their persecutors. In these Catacombs are the graves of many of the martyrs who sealed their sainthood shedding their blood for Christ.

We returned to the States concurrently August 5 aboard Flying Tiger Airlines, landing at New York's Idlewild airport. After picking up the station wagon over in Bayonne, I went to a duty assignment with the National Security Agency (NSA), a Department of Defense intelligence group at Fort Meade, Laurel, Maryland. We took a thirty-day leave in California, then returned to complete a four-year tour with NSA. All functions and responsibilities of NSA are TOP SECRET and cannot be discussed. I can say it was a joint assignment with army, navy, air force, marine, coast guard, and civilian personnel staffing its activities.

We got quarters 1842C, Forrest Avenue, a four-bedroom Wherry Housing apartment complex. It was smaller than the housing we had in Germany, but adequate, even after Monica's birth on September 30, 1958, in the Fort Meade Station Hospital. She received baptism in the post chapel on October 14. A month later, Rosemary was conceived. I started looking for a larger abode.

When I arrived at Fort Meade in August, I immediately entered graduate school at the University of Maryland, College Park, only seven miles away. I had a grade point average of 96.4 in undergraduate study, so I matriculated right away in pursuit of a master degree in History. Attending evening and weekend classes, allowed me to continue full time duty at NSA and to complete all course work for the masters by September 18, 1958. Opportunely, the army that same day approved a "boot strap" program for members pursuing graduate degrees to take extra paid leave, with local commanders' approval, from their duties for up to six months to complete requirements for their degrees.

Program managers both at university and army levels coordinated and evaluated all aspects of the program to insure that

Monica A. Shuffer, 1982.

student attendance, performance, and grades averaging "B" or above. I got both army and university approval to enter the program, and used only four months to research, write, and publish my M.A. thesis entitled: *Development of the U.S. Armored Force 1916–1940.*

The wealth of sources for research and study within easy range of Fort Meade facilitated completion of the thesis. Foremost among these were the University of Maryland Library, the Library of Congress, the National Archives, and the Office of the Chief of Military History at Fort McNair. I relished burying myself in the hearts of these reservoirs of knowledge and fact. Reminiscent of my preschool days when I walked to Mrs. Thompson's first grade with Willetta, I went each weekday with a sack lunch, coffee jug, and writing materials to these fountains of information. I graduated with a Masters Degree in History on January 29, 1959.

Since my USAFI course work, when the army paid two-thirds of tuition costs, I had fully paid all college expenses, beginning with study at Monterey Peninsula College to completion of my masters. This had taken a sizable toll from my pay, but Cecilia and the children had made the sacrifice by lowering living standards to get me through. We employed the formula that I utilized after my enlistment: that is: Live at least two rank pay-grade levels below the grade I held. The difference went to savings or to handle emergencies. As a sergeant, for example, I lived on a Pfc's pay, ignoring inflation; as a major, we got by as first lieutenant's; as a colonel, on a major's salary, etc. We kept this regime, despite our fast growing family. We simply cut frills and went with essentials only. Of course, emergencies made us use savings to meet them, but we thank God that those requiring substantial dips into assets were few and occurred at manageable intervals.

All along we invested regularly, mostly in fixed-income instruments (CDs and annuities). We managed, however, to keep at least three months estimated expenditures in cash accounts. Occasionally, we dabbled into equities, but with spotty success. This performance, though, was due more to my faults of bad analyses and jerky buy and sell transactions. Since retirement, I

107

have done remarkably well with Merrill Lynch managing equity assets.

Cecilia, Gloria, and I received Confirmation in the Catholic faith on June 8, 1958 from Bishop Patrick J. Walsh in Meade's post chapel. David and George III were confirmed in the same chapel by Bishop Walsh on November 29, 1959.

After finishing the masters, I served as assistant director, Society of the Knights of the Altar, training more than 160 altar boys for service in Meade's Catholic chapels. Cecilia and I joined the Third Order of Saint Francis on May 18, 1958 at Holy Name College, Washington, D.C. Priest presiding: Father Stephen D. Hartedgen.

My four-year NSA assignment was the longest tour at one location in my career. Cecilia gave birth to three more children, causing my peers and friends to cry louder for us to quit having babies. "The army is no place for large families," they swore. "You will not get promoted regularly, and you jeopardize your chances for higher schooling. Besides, you restrict your participation in social activities, and this will hurt your efficiency reports."

I neither heard nor saw any such alarm from my superiors and supervisors. Quite the contrary opinion came from them. They applauded my family's growth (these were the baby booming years), praising the children's beauty and conduct. In no way had they noticed my family adversely affecting my duty performance, or my participation in social activities. Thanks to God and Cecilia, our family enhanced, even seasoned, my career and progress.

Neither the army nor the Church takes umbrage at numerous children, if parents can handle them. The Church, in fact, encourages the concept, assigning procreation as the primary purpose of lawful marriage. The true faith especially asks: "Are there any deeds compared to bringing a new life into the world, a life which is to continue for all eternity?" The thing most like God is life, and parents share in God's creative power by bringing a new life into existence.

In the first book of the Bible, God tells us that male and female together are God's image, but God does not leave the matter at that. He exhorts man and woman to increase and multiply to fill the whole world. The harbingers of doom pushing world-wide use of contraceptives to control population to fit their *small,* "humanly" conceived limits, inveigh directly against God's command. They remind me of the Israelites weak in faith, wandering in the desert, doubting if God could "set a table" there to feed them; as if God cannot provide for what He commands.

If male and female together increasing and multiplying to fill the whole world are God's image; then the family that they constitute is God's image. The Christian revelation tells me that God is family. God is Trinity.

The family has been honored throughout history. It is the deepest form of human relations. It is the building block of society. It is the source of the future. It is God's own invention.

Yet, the family is in trouble today, simply by being in America. For there are forces of evil at work in American culture, which make it a child-destroying culture and a family-destroying culture. Because these forces of evil have risen in our time to destroy both the child itself, and the source of both child and family.

The source of both child and family is sex and marriage. Both are under attack. The use of sex is made fruitless by contraception. The divine institution of marriage is put aside by those who want sex without children or commitment. Pregnancy is being separated from birth by abortion. And because these evils are contagious, even good marriages are being infected and destroyed by separation, divorce, and domestic abuse.

In his *Humanae Vitae* encyclical, Pope Paul VI writes that married love is human, total, faithful, exclusive, and creative—truly positive characteristics. For a married couple to experience these values, they must remain close to God and receptive to His will. Contraception represents a rejection of God's assistance; hence a contracepting couple will never realize fully the components of true spousal love.

Moreover, contracepted sex is inherently evil, an offense against God's will for the purpose of human sexuality, and divisive of the two aspects of marriage—the unitive and generative. Under the guise of helping love, contraception cunningly establishes a tyrant in the marriage. The sex act declines from a reaffirming of the whole marriage covenant, true love making, to joint seeking of mutual satisfaction, a subtle shift but a decisive one away from God and the convenant of marriage. Additionally, it opens a pandora's box of more dire ills, such as rogue male behavior, breakup of families, divorce, irreverence for women, cheapening of sex, increased violence and rape, abortion, child abuse, and euthanasia.

In early May 1959, I moved my family into larger quarters at 7763B Nelson Loop, a timely upgrade, because Rosemary came on September 27 (my birthday). She received baptism October 11, in the same chapel where Monica had a year earlier.

I won promotion to major on October 7, continuing as a military intelligence officer at NSA, only now in a supervisory capacity.

Marlene received Confirmation in the faith at St. Mary's Church, Laurel, Maryland, from Bishop Phillip M. Hannan, on October 26, 1960.

Joseph's birth occurred a month later on November 23. Like Monica and Rosemary, he was born in the same hospital and received baptism in the same chapel.

My selection to attend the Command and General Staff College (CG&SC) Regular Course at Fort Leavenworth, Kansas, beginning August 28, 1961, proved my career was seasoning. One needs a continuous string of significantly high performance ratings and potential for the rank of colonel to attend this prestigious institution. CG&SC prepares field-grade officers (major to colonel) to discharge command and general staff duties at organizations from division to field army level. Highly selected officers from other branches of service (navy, air force, and marines) and those from foreign countries of the free world, allied with the United States, also are picked for CG&SC. Class size averages 750 students.

We arrived at Leavenworth as "early birds" in late June, taking quarters 18A, Buckner Drive. It was a stately two-story building with formal living and dining rooms and four bedrooms. Not long after starting CG&SC, I sold my house on Piru Street

Rosemary Shuffer, 1976.

Joseph C. Shuffer, 1983.

for $13,500 and got approval for a Veterans Administration (VA) loan to buy another home.

Maria, born March 27, 1962, was our ninth child. She received baptism on April 7 in the post chapel in Leavenworth.

Rita got confirmed in the Catholic Church at Immaculate Conception Church in Leavenworth from Bishop Edward D. Hunkeller, April 23, 1961.

I graduated from CG&SC on June 12, 1962, number thirty-eight in a class of 752 students. I got picked to take the army's Nuclear Weapons Employment Course (NWEC), which began the day after graduation from CG&SC and lasted a month. The course gave me special qualification to employ battlefield nuclear weapons.

Upon my graduating from NWEC, the army sent us to Taiwan to serve as an advisor to the Republic of China (ROC) Army, reporting on August 8. The orders gave me fifteen days delay en route to visit Cecilia's parents in Los Angeles and mine in Berkeley. GM closed sale of the homestead in Palestine in the late fifties and bought a small apartment house (three apartments) at 1314 Haskell Street in Berkeley. GM and Johnnie lived in the main apartment and rented the other two.

We flew Pan American from San Francisco International airport to Taiwan, passing through Hawaii, and laying over two days in Manila, the Philippines, before landing in Taipei. A typhoon, just ended when we arrived, left the hotel rooms that we occupied with wet floors. We rented number 1 Hsin Hsi Lou, Hsin Peitou for $350, plus utilities monthly (8,750 New Taiwan dollars, affectionately called "NI"). This exceeded a major's housing allowance, which was $297 per month, causing me to rush onto the waiting list for Bank of Taiwan (BOT) housing, which, like regular U.S. government quarters (subsidized), cost only one's housing allowance, and they were better maintained.

The rented house had five bedrooms, two baths, and Chinese decor. It was the largest house that we ever rented. The children especially liked the second bathroom, which eased pressure of morning washups before school. They rode army buses to an excellent elementary school run by Dominican nuns and to

Maria T. Shuffer, 1979.

Taipei American High School conducted by the U.S. Dependent School system.

Service in the Republic of China Military Asssitance Advisory Group (MAAG) required providing training advice and guidance in military tactics and techniques to echelons from division to army levels. Taiwan's army was organized and equipped exactly like the U.S. Army and used U.S. weapons and equipment. My advisory team's escort officer, interpreter, and translator, Major Hsiang Hsi Wu, had graduated from CG&SC two classes before I did. He was superbly motivated and competent to teach tactics for higher commands. We worked with the First ROC Army, headquartered at Chung-li, having the mission to defend the northern half of Taiwan. Lieutenant General Lo Yu-lun, commanding the First Field Army, often praised my team and Major Wu, because we raised combat readiness to superior levels in every division of his army. On June 21, 1963, I graduated from a 120-hour course, taught after duty hours, in Chinese Language, Mandarin Dialect, which facilitated my ability as an advisor to the Chinese. I was already familiar with Chinese Mandarin from a course I took at NSA.

The University of Maryland expanded its overseaes program offering college courses and degree programs in Taiwan, January 1963. My alma mater hired me to teach History, Western Civilization, Management, and Military Logistics. The well-stocked U.S. China MAAG Library near its headquarters, supplemented by the University of Taiwan (Taipei) Library, which had an excellent English section, resourced both teachers and students alike with truly genuine maps and study materials in History, Language, and Mathematics. My History masters qualified me to teach subjects mentioned at college level. During the Taiwan tour, I taught five semesters of American History and Western Civilization. Students completing each course received three units of resident credits, and I got $288 each semester. This was my first civilian pay ever.

On May 1, my number as noted got to the top of the waiting list for BOT housing. We moved from Hsin Peitou to F104, Grass Mountain (U.S. Government quality) housing development overlooking Taipei. It was naturally air conditioned at twenty-five

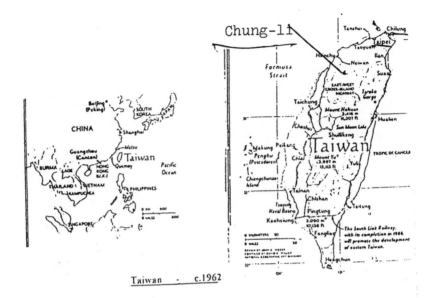

Chung-li

Taipei

Tanshui

Chilung

Taoyuan

Hsinchu

Neiwan

Ilan

Suao

Formosa
Strait

EAST-WEST
CROSS-ISLAND
HIGHWAY

Taroko
Gorge

Taichung

Mount Hohuan
3,416 m
11,207 ft

Hualien

Choshui

Sun Moon Lake

Shuitekeng

Taiwan

Makung

Peikan

Penghu
(Pescadores)

Chiai

Mount Yu
3,997 m
13,113 ft

Yuli

TROPIC OF CANCER

Chuangchunao
Island

Tainan

Chishan

Tsoying
Naval Base

Pingtung

Taitung

Kaohsiung

3,090 m
10,138 ft

Fangliao

— The South Link Railway,
with its completion in 1986,
will promote the development
of eastern Taiwan.

Hengchun

0 KILOMETRE 50

0 MILES 50

DRAWN BY JOHN E. HODES
COMPILED BY EUGENE MILLER
NATIONAL GEOGRAPHIC ART DIVISION

CHINA

Beijing
(Peking)

SOUTH
KOREA

JAPAN

Shanghai

Matsu

Guangzhou
(Canton)

Taiwan

HONG
KONG
(U.K.)

Quemoy

Pacific
Ocean

BURMA

LAOS

THAILAND

VIETNAM

KAMPUCHEA

PHILIPPINES

SINGAPORE

0 KM 800

0 MILES 800

Taiwan   —   c.1962

hundred feet above sea level, and was large, five bedrooms with two baths, and comfortable. We had to purify cooking and drinking water by boiling it, as they did everywhere in Taiwan. We coal-stoked our hot water and furnace heaters more than a few nights in winter, when temperatures surprisingly dropped to 25 degrees Fahrenheit.

Anita's birth on September 7, 1963 happened at the Headquarters, Support Activity (HEDSUPPACT) Naval Hospital in Taiwan at the passing of Typhoon Gloria, the second largest tropical cyclone ever to hit the western Pacific. Luckily, Taipei got only the fringe of the storm, which caused moderate flooding, but little other damage.

Anita received baptism on September 22 in Saint Christopher's Church, Taipei. St. Christopher's served mainly Americans and their dependents in Taipei. Parishioners worked a full week as volunteers, cleaning Gloria's mud and scum from the church before Anita's baptism. Being born a U.S. citizen on foreign soil, she got a Certificate of Citizenship (#AA2422755) issued at Boston, Massachusetts on March 9, 1965.

Military personnel and their dependents surviving the storm cheered at Gloria's passing, for when the flood waters receded, vast quantities of PX and commissary goods, damaged by hail, wind, and water, went on sale at unbelievably low prices. Pairs of expensive women's and men's shoes, unnoticeably harmed, for example, sold for fifty cents. Male and female suits of highest quality, after a good dry cleaning, went for five dollars. Large items, like refrigerators, freezers, and window air conditioners, could be had for under twenty-five. Canned goods, perfectly sound, sold for grab prices of a nickel a can. The most expensive bottles of scotch and liqueurs, whose seals ostensibly protected them, sold for fifty cents. But customers were limited to no more than two items of any commodity. People, nevertheless, stood in lines seemingly a mile long.

I gained promotion to lieutenant colonel on September 25, 1963, and got, for the first time in my career, the remark "general officer material" on my efficiency report. In early December, I won election to the presidency of the Holy Name Society at St.

Anita R. Shuffer, 1985.

Christopher's Church, and Cecilia was chosen Mother of the Year. She was pregnant with Peter at her selection.

The army published orders on February 26, 1964, sending me to the Second Brigade, Fifth Infantry Division at Fort Devens, Ayer, Massachusetts, for duty as battalion commander by August 19. Gloria graduated from Taipei American High School on May 28 and discerned her call to the Catholic Sisterhood. She began processing entry into the Pallottine Order of Religious Sisters in Huntington, West Virginia, by September 10. Cecilia and I thanked God for answering our prayers that our first born would receive a vocation to religious life. Gloria also had been praying and was happily grateful, too.

I persuaded Cecilia to take surface transportation with the children for our return stateside. She was reluctant, being seven months pregnant, to confine herself to cramped spaces aboard a ship plodding along at 12 knots twenty odd days. But she gave in to the children, who were excited with the idea. They bought extra film for their cameras and pictured themselves on deck of a nifty ocean liner. We sailed on the USS *General William Mitchell,* a one-stack troop transport, described by soldiers who had experienced passage aboard her as a veritable "rust bucket." An ocean cruiser? Not. It proved its description true, but calm summer seas gave us a dull, though tolerable, trip with the land of the "big PX" our dominant anxiety.

We departed Chilung (Keelung), Taiwan on July 11, passing through Sasebo and Yokahama, Japan; Honolulu, Hawaii; San Diego and San Francisco, California, to landing at Oakland Army Base on August 2. At each of the stops after landing, we enjoyed a four-hour shopping spree ashore.

During the voyage every crew member did his utmost to comfort passengers, but *Billy Mitchell's* austere trappings struggled to afford it. Hard bunks, designed to sleep combat troops going to war, were horrible substitutes for the soft beds that dependents knew. The dining salon was its only show piece. It had crisp white table cloths, cute curtains at the port holes, and a glistening deck. Waiters served like at Tiffany's. Cecilia, though, had the hardest time taking meals there. *Estaba embarazada* (heavily pregnant), she was not only self-conscious taking her place at the only twelve-person table in the salon, she also detested the curious stares at a family of ten children, and a mother fast gestating number eleven. We survived. Economywise, the entire voyage, lasting twenty-one days, cost only $147.50. Roughly seven dollars a day is not bad at all!

As we approached the mouth of San Francisco Bay at 0400 hours, a freighter in heavy fog side swiped the aft of our vessel port side, jarring everyone awake and crushing two life boats, but caused little other damage. As we passed under that famous bridge at sunrise, the kids had a picture-taking heyday. Tug boats regaled us to landing with musical ship-horn blasts.

8

Vietnam War Experiences

While we were landing at Oakland, North Vietnamese torpedo boats were attacking a U.S. destroyer, U.S. *Maddox,* patrolling international waters in the Gulf of Tonkin off the coasts of North Vietnam and Communist China. The *Maddox* returned fire. Three days later, more enemy gun boats joined the attack. In the days and months following, carrier-based U.S. Navy jet planes attacked torpedo boat bases in North Vietnam, giving birth to a conflict that escalated into a full-blown war between the U.S. and North Vietnam with its Communist guerrilla Vietcong (VC) in the South.

I took command of the Second Battalion, Second Brigade of the Fifth Infantry Division on August 9. No better career-boosting opportunity could have been given me at the time: the chance to lead one of the army's basic maneuver elements in ground combat is a fast developing real war situation. The infantry battalion is a self-contained combat unit of over a thousand men, organized into four companies, and with a full staff to accomplish crucial tasks. It is where savants of military science say, "the buck stops." I was delighted to take the position, but awed, facing the tremendous responsibilities implied.

We moved into quarters 84A Walnut Street at Fort Devens, which were similar to those we had at Leavenworth. The following month I accompanied Gloria to the Pallottines in Huntington. Her face glowed with joy all the way. Coupled with the excitement that teenagers usually feel when leaving home, she was thrilled at beginning a lifetime career, serving the Lord and His people in a most special way. She never looked back. Our hearts tingled as we approached the peaceful, vine-covered con-

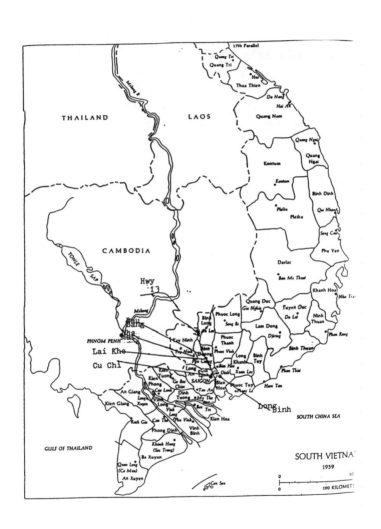

THAILAND

LAOS

17th Parallel

Quang Tri
Quang Tri

Hue
Thua Thien

Da Nang
Hoi An
Quang Nam

Quang Ngai
Quang Ngai

Kontum

Kontum

Binh Dinh
Qui Nhon

Pleiku
Pleiku

Song Cau

Phu Yen

CAMBODIA

Mekong R.

TONLE SAP

Darlac

Ban Me Thuot

Khanh Hoa
Nha Tra

Hwy
13

Quang Duc
Gia Nghia

Tuyen Duc
De Lat

Ninh
Thuan

Mekong

Phuoc Long
Song Be

Lam Dong
Djiring

Binh
Long
An Loc

Phan Rang

Ben
Cat

PHNOM PENH
Tri Tinh

Tay Ninh

Phuoc
Thanh

Binh Thuan

Lai Khe

Tay Ninh
Thuong

Ninh
Phuoc Vinh

Cu Chi

Hau
Nghia

Phan Thiet

Long
Khanh

Binh
Tuy

Kien
Tuong

Go Dau
Duc Hoa

Bien
Hoa

Xuan Loc

Long
An

Di Dinh

Ham Tan

Kien
Phong

Cao Lanh

Dinh
Tuong

Tan An

Bien
Hoa

Phuoc Tuy
Phuoc Le

An Giang

Long
Xuyen

Sa Dec

My Tho

Kien Giang

Long
Vinh

Ben Tre

Dong Binh

Rach Gia

Can Tho

Phu Vinh

Kien Hoa

SOUTH CHINA SEA

Phong Dinh

Vinh
Binh

GULF OF THAILAND

Khanh Hung
(Soc Trang)

Ba Xuyen

Quan Long
(Ca Mau)

An Xuyen

Con Son

SOUTH VIETNAM
1959

0   10
0   100 KILOMETERS

vent sequestered in the hills overlooking the Ohio; our emotions leaped when we saw the nuns lined up to greet us.

Not long after my return to Devens, Peter, our eleventh, was born in the post hospital on October 6. He was registered in the town of Shirley and received baptism in the Catholic chapel at the Massachusetts camp, October 18. Peter's birth weight of eleven pounds destined him to be the tallest of the Shuffers. At age twenty two, he stood at six feet, six inches, where he stands today.

Meanwhile, the Vietnam conflict widened. Following a Vietcong bombardment of an American air base at Pleiku in February 1965, the U.S. retaliated with an air raid on North Vietnam. In the weeks and months that followed, the U.S. stepped up the air war against the North, blasting roads, bridges, storage depots, barracks, railroads, and supply vessels.

This escalation of the air war was matched on the ground. On March 6–9, 3,500 men of the Third Marine Division moved ashore to guard the Danang air base. These were the first U.S. ground combat forces sent to Vietnam. Other marines and army paratroopers followed.

In June, Defense Secretary Robert S. McNamara announced that 21,000 more soldiers were being sent. My battalion was among them.

I had suspected a year before that my battalion would be sent to Vietnam. I began combat training immediately after arriving at Devens. The post is small, compared to other installations quartering infantry troop units, with limited space for battalion-sized units to flex their muscles; so I frequently took my charges to Camp Edwards (fifty miles southeast of Devens) and to the White Mountain training site in New Hampshire (some ninety miles distant) to sharpen their skills. These training sites had terrain characteristics unlike the jungles of southeast Asia, but rugged and dense enough to practice communication and control techniques recommended by U.S. advisors and South Vietnamese units over there. Small unit leaders rehearsed signals and coded messages for moving in extended and contracted formations through difficult areas. Logis-

Peter M. Shuffer, 1982.

tic and medical personnel practiced resupply of ammunition and spare parts and evacuating casualties through dense, low-visibility places. Codes were agreed upon for fire team leaders to equip themselves with colored smoke grenades to mark friendly positions for forward observers and air controllers to fire artillery safely while using air support.

When McNamara's announcement came, my battalion became part of the "Big Red One" (First Infantry Division) and received the designation: Second Battalion, Second Infantry (2/2, popularly known as the "Double Devils" in a fight). I got orders to take the "devils" to Vietnam for battle no later than September 20. This alert came on August 15. Once again I had to move, settle my family, register kids in school, and fly to an Asian battlefield for combat. Only this time I had to move a combat-ready battalion over there in the same short time frame, and Cecilia was not pregnant.

I tried to buy a home in Fitchburg, Leonminster, and Ayer (locales near Devens), but I could not find one suitable to our means and needs. We found no racially prejudiced covenants where houses were available that barred blacks. Black population density in central Massachusetts was minuscule to nonexistent (excepting military bases). Then too, the Civil Rights Acts of 1964–65 prohibited constrictive covenants denying minorities rights to purchase homes for sale based on skin color or ethnic origin.

Opportunely, the army found excess family quarters at Fort Lewis, Washington, for field-grade officers deploying to Vietnam. Our family got 2660D Fifth Street, quarters that were identical to those at Devens.

David graduated from St. Bernard's High School in Fitchburg on June 13 and won acceptance at Brescia College in Owensboro, Kentucky. Brescia was an excellent Catholic college, which offered him fields of study that he desired. On August 27, he departed for Brescia. The next day I took the remainder of the family by station wagon to Fort Lewis, arriving on September 1.

By that time Communist VC and North Vietnamese Army (NVA) units had stepped up the pace of their attacks, gradually overrunning and occupying large areas of South Vietnam. In

Saigon the war-weary South Vietnam government was racked with an almost unending succession of cabinet crises, military coups, and countercoups.

I returned by air to Devens on September 3, and I moved my battalion less an advanced party (twenty officers and men) to Boston Navy Base where they embarked for shipment to Vietnam. Transiting via the Panama Canal Zone, they made their deadline on time.

Taking the advanced party to Hanscom AFB, Massachusetts, I moved them by C-130 aircraft to the war zone, departing Continental U.S. from McCord AFB, Washington, and arriving at Long Binh on September 10. When we landed, we observed aircraft defoliating the surrounding jungle with Agent Orange almost daily. To date, I have experienced no adverse health problems due to the sprayings.

Ship-borne elements of 2/2 joined me in the Long Binh staging area on September 20. Together with the Third Brigade, we established a base camp perimeter at Lai Khe in the Michelin Rubber Plantation, which lay astride Highway 13 between Phu Coung and An Loc. My mission was to conduct search-and-destroy operations in Tay Ninh, Biah Long, and Binh Duong Provinces—home ground of the 272nd and 273rd VC regiments and their separate Phu Loi Battalion. Additionally, I secured Highway 13 for passage of American and Allied units on order.

Study and analysis of the weather, enemy, and terrain in our area of operations confirmed my previous findings that once a battle is joined, firepower will dominate maneuver of ground forces as the choice instrument for victory. Indeed, infantry units today have more firepower available than in any previous war. Air Force high-level bombers and low-level fighters, helicopter gun ships, and artillery of assorted caliber stand ready in larger quantities than ever before to help the ground fighter.

The infantryman himself, with improved weapons and communication, can overwhelm most opponents, if he uses his immediate firepower properly. This analysis proved true in my battalion's major victories, the battles of Ap Bau Bang, November 12, 1965, and Ap Nha Mat, December 5.

At Bau Bang, I had the mission to secure Highway 13 from Lai Khe to the Tay Ninh Province boundary for the Seventh South Vietnamese (ARVN) Division to pass into Tay Ninh for search and destroy operations. Enemy troops in the area were the 272nd Regiment west of Highway 13 and the Phu Loi Battalion southeast of Bau Bang. I had Troop A, 1/4 Cavalry, mounted in armored personnel carriers (APC's) and Battery C, Thirty-third Artillery (towed) attached. My battalion was dismounted.

At 1500 hours, November 11, I declared the artery clear, and the Seventh ARVN moved through without incident. Afterward, I decided to coil in a night defense perimeter on a high mound, clearing approximately three hundred yards in diameter on the northern edge of Bau Bang. The position gave superior observation and fields of fire in daylight, but it was less than satisfactory for night defense. Nevertheless, I continued establishing entrenchment on the mound, while curious Ban Bang villagers, some suspected VC in civilian dress, looked on. A few young girls sold cold soft drinks to my sweaty GIs digging in the steamy afternoon sun. I was unhappy with the mound location, because my outer perimeter was too close to the surrounding jungle edge and the village to provide acceptable fields of fire and observation in darkness. Besides, my men on the mound would be silhouetted for VC emerging from the jungle background.

In the meantime, I dispatched secret reconnaissance parties south to a large pea patch over five hundred yards in diameter and level. Pea stalks were uniformly four to five feet high, offering excellent concealment, even for the APCs and artillery pieces. I had observed the site from the helicopter used in the road-clearing operation the day before. I infiltrated eight APCs into traffic on 13 to the pea patch with instructions to detach their rear doors and use tow cables to drag a two-hundred-yard wide swath clearing around the outer edge to give us good concealment and night observation and a killing zone all around the position. Cerise air-ground panels at measured intervals along the concertina around the position gave unmistakable identity to my "devils" for air controllers and artillery observers. My CP was in dead center of the position with a cleared helicopter landing zone for air evacuation of casualties and resupply of ammunition and spare parts. My jeep with excellent radios stood camouflaged, operating with extended transmitter/receiver cables to my foxhole. At 0230 hours, November 12, the 272nd enemy regiment attacked the empty dugouts on the mound north of Bau Bang. It was 0500 hours before they realized we were in the pea patch, and the first streaks of dawn were breaking before they could change assault direction against the patch.

I had prepared Company B, which was three miles north of the village still guarding 13 for ARVN traffic, to rejoin the battalion. When the attack began, I alerted Company B to attack south on order to hit the VC forces from the rear in Bau Bang.

Elements of the Phu Loi Battalion were already based in jungle areas southeast and southwest of the village to harass and interdict Allied traffic on 13. At 0600 hours, mortar rounds from these units began falling on us in the patch initiating the attack (arrow one on page 131). The attack was repulsed. The second attack (arrow two on page 131) supported by heavier mortar, and recoilless rifle fire was also beaten off by intense counter-fire before it reached the concertina wire.

Subsequently, the VC made their deepest penetration of the day (arrow three) when they got close enough to lob grenades into powder bags of one of the artillery howitzers. The gun crew, using direct fire together with heavy perimeter machine gun fire, hurled the enemy back with heavy casualties.

Before the VC attacked the mound, villagers fled Bau Bang north along 13, and the enemy occupied it. After the third attack was thrown back, the insurgents committed their heaviest assault of the day (arrow four). This move was a desperate frontal, suicidal push into withering short-range fire from Company A and a platoon of cavalry, shooting .50-caliber machine guns mounted on the APCs. They failed to get to the concertina wire. Heavy artillery rounds from support batteries at Lai Khe fell in the killing zone ringing our perimeter. Enemy efforts weakened and bounced counterclockwise along our position until they faded into the woods to the northwest.

Then the air force and helicopter gun ships took over, while artillery pounded enemy avenues of escape. Fighter jets savaged

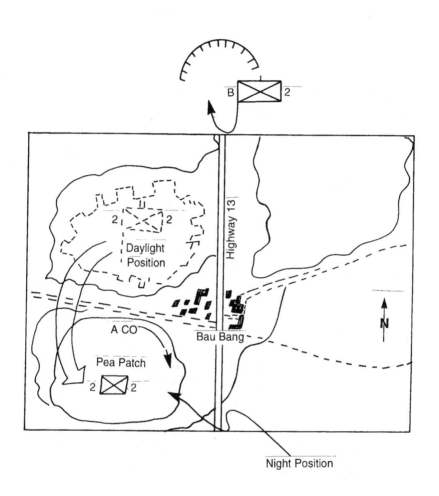

B ⊠ 2

2 ⌐1⌐ 2

Daylight
Position

Highway 13

2

A CO

Pea Patch

Bau Bang

2 ⊠ 2

N

Night Position

disorganized VC with napalm, cluster bomb units (CBU's), rockets, and heavier bombs. Air force firepower also killed the VC, who tried to hide in the village.

At 12:30 P.M., the 2/2 won the day. Immediately thereafter, my once-surrounded charges counterattacked from the perimeter and swept in a clockwise movement through the jungle to the northwest, into the village, and back to the pea patch. Air sorties harried the enemy retreat, while artillery continued to blast their avenues of escape.

We counted 198 VC killed and estimated killing 200 more. My "devils" captured two wounded VC. Among the hundreds of articles left behind by the insurgents were over 500 rounds of small arms ammunition, 51 individual weapons, 10 machine guns, 7 recoilless rifles, 3 Chinese flame throwers, and a small cannon. I lost twenty killed and forty-six wounded. For the victory, the battalion won a Valorous Unit Citation from Secretary Robert McNamara, and was recommended for the Presidential Unit Citation. I got my third Silver Star Medal, two air medals for gallantry in action, and a third award of the Combat Infantryman Badge. The air medals were given for the numerous hours of helicopter reconnaissance and surveillance for the battalion, clearing 13 before the battle.

The main lesson learned was the value of individual infantrymen firing their weapons timely, rapidly, and accurately during enemy assaults. The first five minutes of a VC attack are the most critical, because Communist guerrillas will do their utmost, especially in daylight, to "hug" you quickly, to escape the fury of superior American mortar, artillery, and aircraft fire. Another key lesson was the importance of careful analysis of the terrain and lighting conditions in selecting defensive positions and/or avenues of approach in offensive actions. This is a signal factor ground into me from my Korean experiences.

Cover and concealment, observation and fields of fire, also rise in priority value, especially for defenders. Another valuable note is to keep soda pop vendors and curious civilians away from selected positions. They, more often than not, are spies who will tell the enemy where your automatic weapons and heavier guns are located.

Blow By Blow Account Tells Bau Bang Story

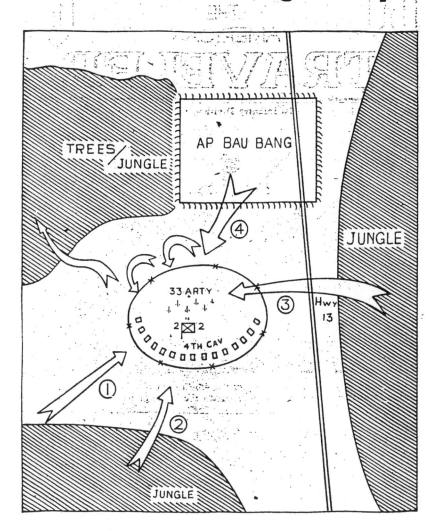

Three weeks after Bau Bang, my battalion was searching the dense jungle area hiding the Long Nguyen Secret Zone thirty-five miles north of Saigon. This long established VC hideout overlaid the boundaries of Tay Ninh, Binh Long, and Binh Duong Provinces, and it was the breeding ground of the 272nd and 273rd Regiments. It was also a favorite assembly area and way station for main force Communist units moving between War Zones C and D. The Seventh ARVN was overrun during late November on the western edge of the Michelin Rubber Plantation by Red Viet forces, which had trained, staged, and jumped off from Long Nguyen.

Vietcong throughout the area had been elusive since their defeat at Bau Bang and their victory over the Seventh ARVN later in November. Their disappearance was especially frustrating to me, because of the "nickel and dime" casualties that we were suffering from mines, punji traps, local snipers, and the humid, dehydrating jungle heat during searches.

Unknown to us was the meticulously camouflaged 272nd and 273rd base camp just a mile south of our overnight perimeter and astride our route of advance (Figure 1).

Enemy morale was high, although his supplies were low because of recent strenuous battles and the difficulty of resupplying in the short time lapse since previous engagements.

We moved out south at 0805 hours, December 5, parallel to a north-south jungle road, sweeping with Companies B and C abreast and Company A in reserve as rear guard and ground reaction force (Figure 2).

It was almost noon before lead elements made enemy contact. As we neared the camp, VC, practicing "hugging tactics," rushed out of their craftily fortified position in force to meet us. Several Chinese-manufactured 12.7 millimeter machine guns covered enemy movements from tall tree-mounted platforms. Companies B and C were pinned down instantly. Artillery at Lai Khe promptly responded to our request for fire on the base camp.

Initial analysis revealed that the VC west flank was weakest; so I committed Company A in a sweep around this flank. This move was stopped by stronger VC elements, which tried to hug it.

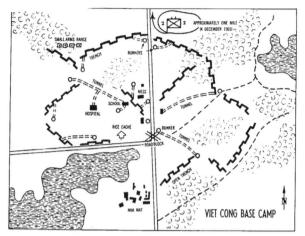

Figure 1.

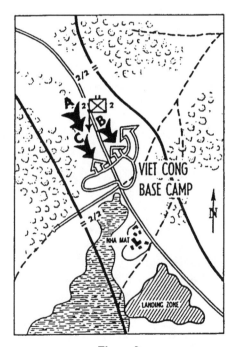

Figure 2.

Meantime, Company B, taking moderate casualties, fell back to the west shoulder of the road, refusing its flank, which provided them adequate cover to deliver increased, accurate fire. This stopped the main attack temporarily. Battalion CP elements deployed thinly across the north flank to complete the best perimeter defense under the circumstances. The refuge of numerous laterite ant hills, three feet high and an arm's length thick, together with very rapid small arms fire, prevented hand-to-hand combat with the VC advances. Pinned down and surrounded in a dense jungle, my "devils" held and depended on coordinated superior firepower, delivered from above the jungle canopy, to win the day.

Colonel William Brodbeck, Third Brigade Commander, gave me priority of all available air and artillery fires and alerted air-mobile (Second Battalion, Twenty-eighth Infantry) for movement on order to a selected landing zone just south of Nha Mat. One battery each of 105 millimeter, 155 millimeter, and eight-inch artillery, three helicopter gun teams, and forty-three sorties of fighter aircraft were available. Optimum use of this formidable arsenal required careful coordination and unmistakable description of friendly forces and target areas. Simultaneous employment of all these supporting fires would produce the best results (Figure 3).

The most pressing threat came from the stirring two-battalion enemy force east of the road endangering Company B. Air force fighter jets were assigned this target area, suggesting that planes stay east of the road to leave clear fields for the artillery to the west. Fire team leaders equipped with colored smoke grenades marked Company B's lines. This unit had brought its wounded with them when they were forced west of the road. Air force bombs, of course, had to be dropped a safe distance from the road, but CBU's, 20mm cannon, and napalm could be used almost to the road's east shoulder.

The well-entrenched base camp complex opposite Companies A and C, together with the tree snipers and machine guns, were engaged by artillery. The light battery was already firing on these targets. Additionally, the area was south of my charges, permitting safe, uninterrupted fire from guns of all cali-

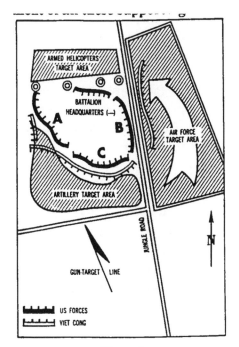

Figure 3.

ber at Lai Khe. An aerial observer quickly adjusted these fires. This allowed Companies A and C to resume forward movement.

Armed helicopters took the north flank. Several VC infiltrators had moved around to cut off suspected friendly reinforcements from the north and to harass CP elements. Flying just above the canopy and guided by smoke grenades, the flying gun ships delivered their rockets and machine gun fire in area coverage against the infiltrators.

For almost four hours, this dreadful armory hung a virtual curtain of fire around my men. The entire area shook as the fighter bombers broke the back of the VC attack. Radio messages from A and C companies confirmed their assault against the heart of the camp. My CP group followed close on their heels.

With their ammunition exhausted and their main fighting soldiers killed or wounded, the VC broke and ran, leaving their dead, weapons, and equipment scattered over the battlefield. Artillery forward observers and air controllers pursued them relentlessly with their fires. Brodbeck attached Company C, 28th to me. It landed in the selected zone to assist in destroying the camp and policing the battlefield.

We remained in the VC camp three days, not only destroying it, but also denying the Communists use of their favorite liaison and supply routes between War Zones C and D. Brodbeck scheduled the area for continued surveillance and targeted it for harassing and interdictory fires from Lai Khe. On two occasions, after the battle, my men drove off several VC porters and logistic persons returning to scavenge the battle site. (Had American forces been reinforced with more ground troops to hold captured, critical areas like the base camp to physically deny enemy use, the war might have ended differently. Instead, we kept searching and destroying to defeat an elusive, but determined enemy, who was deterred by firepower, but not denied use of key areas.) VC casualties totaled 301 known dead, and 300 more estimated killed. We captured seven enemy soldiers, four 2 1/2 ton truck loads of weapons and ammunition, hospital supplies, and 12 tons of rice. I lost 40 killed, 104 wounded, and 1 missing. We got another Valorous Unit Citation, and I received the Legion of Merit and the Vietnamese Gallantry Cross with Silver Star.

136

After-action reports confirmed all the lessons learned at Bau Bang. Perhaps the central teaching from both battles is the significance of making coordinated use of supporting firepower when the enemy is located and fixed.

Late in February 1966, after the enemy escaped my grasp in a desultory action near Cu Chi, I got word of my selection to attend the U.S. Army War College beginning August 28. I took an interim assignment in March to II Field Force, an army corps, which had the southern half of South Vietnam as its area of operation. I served as G-2 operations officer until June, when I prepared to leave Vietnam. For my performance at II Field Force, I got my third Bronze Star Medal.

Retrospectively, I realized several "firsts" in the Vietnam conflict. For the first time, white and black U.S. soldiers *began* a war fighting in fully integrated units from fire team to army level. Foremost, too, senior black officers successfully commanded subordinate white officers in field and staff positions. Unlike previous wars when some white officers blamed all-black units in the line for their defeat and mission failure, integrated outfits had higher morale and stronger cohesion in the fray, seeming to forgot skin color and embrace teamwork to win. Moreover, integrated teams had, previous to deployment, trained together, with whites and blacks getting accustomed to seeing one another doing the same thing and doing it well—together!

Shortly after 2/2 arrived in country, the city of Fitchburg, Massachusetts, "adopted" the Double Devils, pledging its whole-hearted support. The *Fitchburg Sentinel* published "Chamber to aid Viet GI's," adopting my unit. (See copy of article page 139.)

Numerous cities across our land have done this for various units in previous wars, but this was a first for me in my three-war experience. From the outset, I discouraged the chamber and all supporters from sending "items" to my charges, because the army adequately supplies all its soldiers with their combat needs. I instead asked for their prayers and "pen pal" type relationships with my men.

Also unique in my "Nam" experience was having Chaplain

(First Lieutenant, now deceased) Thomas Miller, a Roman Catholic priest as my battalion chaplain. Lean, tall, and somber with penetrating eyes, Father Tom, a redheaded Irish-American of quick wit and profound wisdom, endeared himself to the heart of every Double Devil. Father Tom stayed active with the men all the time. He often begged his way aboard "Hueys" taking hot chow to fighting men in dangerous jungle positions and frequently rode "dust off" choppers, gathering wounded from precarious landing zones. Every time he went, he would try to celebrate Holy Mass in the safest area around.

With the help of attached engineers, my troops built Father a rubber tree log chapel (seating seventy-five) in the Lai Khe base. Upward of forty men, some Protestant, attended his 6:00 A.M. daily Mass. My men found great comfort and security praying with him.

Another "first" event, in my view, was the parade of VIPs visiting my battalion.

Senator Henry M. "Scoop" Jackson (D) Washington, and Chairman of the Senate Armed Forces Committee; Representative Edward P. Boland (D) Massachusetts, and Chairman of the House Armed Forces Committee; Representative Olin E. Teague (D) Texas, representing the Eighth District (Palestine); Secretary of the Army, Stanley Resor; Lieutenant General Nguyen Van Thieu, President of South Vietnam; General William C. Westmoreland, Commanding General, Military Allied Command, Vietnam (MACV); and Major General (later Lieutenant General) Jonathan C. Seaman, Commanding General, "Big Red One," First Infantry Division. They all came to congratulate and inspire the 2/2.

Chamber To Aid Viet GI's

William B. Giadone, president of the Fitchburg Chamber of Commerce, today enlisted the chamber's aid in collecting articles for area soldiers in Viet Nam.

Upon receipt of a letter from Mrs. Eileen Gallant of 355 Beech St., the chamber is establishing itself as a collection point for articles to be donated. Its address is 781 Main St., second floor.

The text of Mrs. Gallant's letter follows.

"Dear sir, I would like to ask the Fitchburg Chamber of Commerce a favor for the boys in Viet Nam.

"You see, a month ago a few housewives and myself sent a package over to the Second Battalion, Second Infantry, a group that had been stationed at Fort Devens. Since then, I have received about 30 letters from the boys over there, and believe me, they really appreciate the mail as well as the packages.

"I've even met one of the wives who lives in a trailer park in Lunenburg. After talking to her, I've suddenly realized just how much these boys need over there — everything from soap and toilet articles and shaving equipment of clothes and underwear.

"Understandably, these boys want and need and appreciate these things, as well as cookies and special goodies that people send at Christmas.

"So the favor I'd like to ask the Chamber of Commerce is: please ask the merchants of this city to donate anything they can think of, as these boys can use whatever you can think of.

"We girls are going to send another package over soon, so if you'd like to join us, or if you'd prefer, I can give you the address and you can send it yourself. However you choose, the men of the 2/2 will be sure to know that the city of Fitchburg has adopted them, and that we support them wholeheartedly.

"Please gentlemen, while they are over there being shot at and killed, let's tell them we care and truly appreciate them and what they're doing."

The chamber officials note that gifts by anyone will be accepted at their receiving point, not only gifts by chamber members. Persons wanting to donate money for postage fees on the articles are encouraged to do so.

A partial list follows of the articles found most useful and best liked by the men in Viet Nam: underwear, shaving and hair cream, shampoo, toothpaste and brushes, aspirins, deodorants, razors, blades, soap, boot socks, insect repellent, pop corn, vitamins, presweetened instant drinks, presweetened cereal and crossword puzzles.

Other items: shoe laces, suntan lotion, writing paper, gum, games, paper plates, fruits, fruit cakes, dairy coffee cream, foot powder, shoe polish, books, envelopes, c a n d y, greeting cards, needles, baking soda, napkins, sugar cubes, tea bags, instant coffee, shoe brushes, playing cards, pens, cough drops, handkerchiefs, thread, coffee cakes and spiced cakes.

Senator Henry M. "Scoop" Jackson visiting the 2/2, November 1965. LTC George M. Shuffer second from left.

Congressman Edward P. Boland visiting the 2/2, November 1965. LTC George M. Shuffer second from left.

Congressman Olin E. Teague visiting the 2/2 at Lai Khe, November, 1965. LTC George M. Shuffer in center.

LTG Nguyen Van Thieu, President of South Vietnam, visiting LTC Shuffer at 2/2, November, 1965.

Secretary of the Army Stanley Resor visiting the 2/2, November, 1965. LTC George M. Shuffer immediately right of Resor.

Major General Jonathan C. Seaman, Commander, 1st Inf. Div., congratulating officers and men of the 2/2, November, 1965. LTC George M. Shuffer, right of Seaman.

General William C. Westmoreland, Commander MACV, visiting the 2/2, November, 1965. LTC George M. Shuffer on Westmoreland's left.

LTC George M. Shuffer directing counterattack sweep after victory at Bau Bang, November 12, 1965.

9

The Senior Years

On June 16, 1966, I flew from Ton Son Nhut AFB, Saigon, to Travis AFB, California. A short air-hop the next day up to Seattle and Fort Lewis reunited me with my family for a thirty-day leave and countless prayers of thanksgiving for getting home safely.

After the leave, we moved by station wagon to Carlisle Barracks, Carlisle, Pennsylvania, home of the U.S. Army War College, where we occupied quarters 541 Craig Road on August 5. The Army War College embodies the ultimate education for military officers. It prepares them to formulate national strategy and make decisions in military operational matters of U.S. concern. During attendance there, I was a member of the Community Speakers Bureau, and I made speeches to colleges, schools, clubs, and civic groups throughout central Pennsylvania on topics of current interest. I also won election to the Executive Committee of the Holy Name Society (an organization committed to fostering reverence for God and His name), and published "Finish Them with Firepower" in the *Military Review,* December 1967.

George III graduated from Trinity High School, Carlisle, on May 29, 1967, and gained appointment to the U.S. Naval Academy and the class of 1971. He also was accepted at the Air Force, Coast Guard, and Merchant Marine academies, and was in the "hole" of the selection process to West Point and the Military Academy. I recommended that he wait for the call to West Point, a chancy idea that would have fructified only if a regular selected fell out. He chose the navy instead, and I blessed his choice.

In addition to providing the military officer studying national strategy the highest possible military education, the War

146

College's research element thoroughly trains students in research techniques and analysis of military strategies. In the process, students are required to research, analyze, and write an essay on warfare strategy as a requirement for graduation. At the time, the U.S. Army was deeply involved in the Vietnam conflict, in which the objective was to defeat the enemy militarily. My essay attempted to show that we not only needed to defeat the insurgents' military, but also we needed to win the hearts and minds of the Vietnamese people. The essay analyzed Vo Nguyen Giap's (North Vietnam's military leader) revolutionary warfare strategy and tactics from a counterinsurgent's point of view. The analysis indicated that Giap's strategy pattern was based on a slowly escalating conflict in which insurgent forces erode superior enemy power while garnering influence to themselves. Giap's insurgents grew on peasant support gained by polico-military activities and organization. The main thrust throughout the struggle was on the psychological aspects of war to win the population. The best countermeasures against this strategy, I concluded, lay in this vein, because ultimate counterinsurgent victory depends on winning the approval of the population.

After graduation from the War College on June 12, 1967, I went to army staff duty at the Pentagon in the Office of Deputy Chief of Staff for Military Operations (ODCSOPS). There I gave briefings, made staff studies, and wrote action papers for decision making on military matters of national interest. Specifically, I was the assigned troop operations branch chief, supervising seven action officers and four secretaries/typists, managing plans and operations in the Troop Operations Division, Operations Directorate, ODCSOPS. I was the operative for actions pertaining to nuclear weapons dispersal, deployments, and status; controlled fragmentation munitions and special weapons; and strategic offensive forces. I was also responsible for initiating and developing army views concerning manned space flight support, worldwide emergency evacuation of non-combatants, arms control and disarmament, mobilization, strategic mobility, joint exercises, intelligence, and army aviation.

We bought 711 North Belgrade Road, Silver Spring, Maryland, for $29,500 as our family residence. It had four bedrooms, living and dining rooms, kitchen, one and a half baths, a patio and large back yard. The children attended excellent Montgomery County schools. We were members of St. Andrew's Catholic Church and were chosen Family of the Year for the Archdiocese of Washington in October 1968 (Family pictured with Archbishop Patrick J. O'Boyle).

At the Pentagon, I received the Army Commendation Medal and the Army General Staff Identification Badge for meritorious performance of my assignment with ODCSOPS.

Remaining at the Pentagon, I became a military assistant in the Office of the Secretary of Defense, the highest staff position of my career. I worked with the Director of Organization and Management Planning, Office of the Assistant Secretary of Defense (Administration). Conducting research and developing plans for managing and organizing the Department of Defense, to improve its performance, gave me valuable Joint Staff experience, as I coordinated staff actions with counterpart officers of the navy, air force, marines, and coast guard. Together we prepared presentations on organizational and management problems to be used within the Department of Defense and for the Executive Office of the President and the Congress.

I got promoted to colonel on August 28, three days before Johnnie's eightieth birthday. She was overwhelmed with pride and joy, running about bragging, "My baby is a colonel of the U.S.!" I was happy, too, and grateful for God's blessings. My performance in the Office of the Secretary of Defense brought my second Legion of Merit and the Office of the Secretary of Defense Identification Badge. I also published "An Appropriate Response," in the *Military Review,* December 1969.

David graduated, Distinguished ROTC Graduate, from the University of Maryland with a Bachelor of Arts Degree in History on June 7 and was commissioned a second lieutenant, U.S. Air Force. He had gotten a private pilot's license in Silver Spring in April; so the air force ordered him to active duty and sent him to Randolph AFB, Texas, for regular air force pilot training.

Marlene graduated from Northwood High School in Silver

Picture of my family with Archbishop Patrick J. O'Boyle, as Family of the Year 1968, at the Immaculate Conception Shrine, Washington D.C., October, 1968. Top row, left to right: George Shuffer III (Midshipman, U.S. Naval Academy), David K. Shuffer (2nd Lieutenant, USAF), Colonel George M. Shuffer, Jr. (Infantry), the Archbishop, Mrs. Shuffer, Sr. Gloria, Rita, Marlene. Bottom row, left to right: Peter, Joseph, Anita, Monica, Maria, and Rosemary.

Spring on June 20 and became a freshman at the University of Maryland in September.

Just before Christmas, I got orders sending me to Headquarters, U.S. Army South (Panama) to take command of the 193rd Infantry Brigade by April 15, 1970. My family planned to remain in Silver Spring until the school term ended that year.

Arriving in the Canal Zone on April 15, I took leadership of the 193rd, the only significant ground fighting force south of the U.S. border. My mission was to defend the Canal against any threat to passage of ships of all nations, and the right of the U.S. to operate the Canal. I had a secondary mission to rescue U.S. noncombatants from unchecked violence and attack in the capitals of all nations of Central and South America. My brigade had three infantry battalions (one armored personnel carrier mounted), an airborne infantry company, an artillery battery, and a combat engineer company.

I found the brigade below C-1 (the top rating for combat readiness) in personnel, training, and maintenance. I took immediate action to raise these critical areas to C-1 rating. This called for bringing specialty qualification (MOS) personnel to required strength, added daily training and work hours (no more automatic Saturdays off), and closer supervision of maintenance of weapons, vehicles, aircraft, and equipment. Commander, U.S. Army South (USARSO) Major General Chester L. Johnson and his staff supported me 100 percent.

In less than sixty days, the brigade sported a C-1 in all readiness categories. Troop morale soared, giving point to the adage: "Soldiers made to soldier, quickly learn to embrace army life."

At age forty-six and entering my thirty-first year of infantry service, I applied for airborne training. I did not have to. There was no criterion for the brigade commander to be airborne qualified. But I wanted to lead all elements of my command in execution of their mission(s), and this included the airborne company, which plays a critical role in rescuing noncombatants from dangerous situations. The Eighth Special Forces Airborne School in the Canal Zone gladly scheduled my training.

But the weightiest problem in the brigade was growing vol-

150

untary polarization of blacks and whites, especially after duty hours in social, athletic, and recreational activities. Group race arguments and contentions also increased. Complaints arose from what blacks perceived as unequal justice that they received compared to whites in punishments for infractions. Blacks also thought they were unfairly passed over in deference to whites for promotion and higher schooling opportunities.

After centuries of discrimination and "last" class status, black soldiers saw President Truman's integration order and the favorable court rulings and congressional enactments of the fifties and sixties as glowing promises of equal opportunity in a truly integrated military. The ongoing Vietnam War demonstrated that fully integrated units under good leadership performed better than all-black units in previous wars. The horrors of battle, the desire to win and come home alive, blotted out considerations of hair texture and skin color, even among white/black foxhole buddies.

Now, back in garrison life, blacks visualized and expected warm white embrace of acceptance as equal military professionals. Instead they collided with the same white racism and rejection that they had known before, only this time they were excluded, not as units, but as individuals in close proximity. Black soldiers retaliated, rejecting whites, reasoning: "Whitey doesn't want us, and we don't want whitey." Results: Two separate hostile camps in a single military unit. Wrong way!

Race harmony, then, loomed among the highest priority missions that I had to accomplish. Without it, I was sure to fail along with the unit. Race harmony occurs when the races volunteer in their hearts and minds to live and work *together* as equals in *all* aspects of life—social, economic, political, military, and spiritual.

This awesome mission is difficult, but not impossible to accomplish. It takes much prayer, faith, and round-the-clock, concerned leadership at every link in the chain of command. I achieved it by:

Devising, writing, and widely publishing a Equal Opportunity/Race Harmony Program in the brigade, declaring in the preamble: Racism, white or Black, and segregation (also polarization) are forbidden, no matter who instigates or promotes them. Copies of the full program were affixed to every bulletin board in the command. Then, "Commander's Talks," with all members present, were held to explain the program's purpose and objectives, and the commander's unequivocal belief in and determination to enforce them without exception. Commander's or leader's talks were made by commanders and leaders and never delegated.

The program included:

Policy to provide equal enforcement of military justice, including penalties and punishments for all offenders, regardless of race or ethnicity.

Guaranteed equal opportunity for advanced schooling and promotion for all members: that is, commanders were to closely monitor promotion selection procedures, and provide additional training and education after duty hours to assist the disadvantaged and unqualified to qualify, and not just to qualify, but also to achieve the ends of their qualifications. This was not "affirmative action." It was positive, determined effort by commanders to develop potential, which is there, but barred from bearing fruit, because of circumstances beyond the possessor's control.

Strong discouragement of racial polarization after duty hours and flatly forbid it on duty, insisting that every unit, large or small, and all aspects of its function be thoroughly integrated. I forbade all-black and all-white teams from competing in intramural sports and marksmanship activities.

I forbade verbal expressions and display of slogans, flags, emblems, and propaganda with racial innuendoes anywhere in the brigade area and strongly protested their publication in surrounding areas.

I positively encouraged white-black togetherness, making it clear this was my aim and desire. Subordinates got the message and were inclined to comply, whether they saw all the reasons or none of them. Not that I wanted members to become racial zombies, but I desired them to be fully informed that I firmly believed that togetherness enhances unit effectiveness, esprit, and morale.

Troops customarily do what the commander desires. The

193rd complied. Racial tension practically disappeared, and harmony reigned.

I firmly believe that American soldiers of all races and origins of birth will accept such a program. Some because they have no choice. Most because deep in their hearts, they harbor the dream of making ours an army, as Martin Luther King dreamed, "where men and women are judged by the content of their character, and not by the color of their skin."

Fortunately, the Canal Zone and Latin America remained calm and peaceful during my eighteen-month command tour. Panama's President, General Omar Torrijos Herrera, while unhappy with America controlling postal service for Panamanians living in the Canal Zone and the amounts of revenue that his country received from canal operations, nevertheless kept Panama in compliance with the treaty ratified in 1939, which set revenue amounts and gave the U.S. the rights to handle postal service for his countrymen living in the Zone.

Rita graduated from Northwood High School in Silver Spring on June 17, 1970. Three days later, my family arrived in the Canal Zone and occupied quarters at 301, Fort Kobbe. Marlene, who had completed her freshman year at Maryland, joined Rita in attending Canal Zone College for the 1970–71 college year. My other children at home went to Catholic parochial schools there.

In October 1970, George III resigned from the Naval Academy and boarded aircraft carrier USS *Roosevelt* for enlisted service with the Sixth Fleet in the Mediterranean. After completing three years at the academy, he realized that navy and military service were not his forte. Navy regulations require midshipmen, who resign after two years and before graduation, to serve at least two years in the enlisted ranks of the fleet before discharge; so George III went to the Mediterranean, where he could contribute his best.

Marlene married Air Force Sergeant Robert Hermann Kuhn at Howard AFB, Canal Zone Catholic Chapel on May 29, 1971. Bob and Marlene departed Panama in early June to an assignment at Hill AFB, Utah (Bob's terminal assignment in the air force). In 1972, he entered the University of Illinois to acquire a masters in Civil Engineering. After graduation in 1974, he became the City Engineer of Muskegon, Michigan.

I received an offer to sell my house at 711 North Belgrade Road in Silver Spring, which I had rented out while in Panama. Accepting the offer, I sold it for $37,000, on July 12. The next day Johnnie died, and I sadly took leave to bury her. Returning to the Canal after the funeral, I entered the Eighth Special Forces Airborne School for parachutist training. Anticipating this rigorous pursuit, I spent the previous month running two and a half miles daily before breakfast. I also did 75 pushups and 30 sit-ups, all in a thirty-minute period. Running early morning in August on Balboa Heights where our quarters sat, I often saw the Big Dipper at one end of the sky and the Southern Cross at the other, an unusual astral combination in the skies over the U.S., but common in Panama and at sites near the equator. Military policemen often mistook me for a skinny Panamanian burglar, who recently had raided officers' row. I was frequently stopped in the first week running for identification checks; so I habitually carried my ID card even in shorts and T-shirt.

Making five required jumps for the Airborne Badge, I was superb on jumps one and two, landing perfectly each time. We made jump three the next day in winds at the maximum allowable speed of eight miles per hour for training jumps. I made a violent swing landing on the embankment of a roadway through the drop zone. Stupidly, I put out my right elbow to arrest the vicious roll after hitting the ground. The shoulder dislocation that resulted took most of the night getting it back into its socket. Back to duty the next day in a body cast, I was embarrassed, returning salutes with my left hand. I got the doctor to cut off the cast after ten days and took painful but successful physical therapy to regain normal use of my shoulder and arm in ten more days.

Determined to finish all qualifying jumps right away, I got permission to make the final two jumps into Gatun Lake (a soft landing drop zone). They went well, and I qualified, graduating from airborne school and receiving the Parachute Badge on October 4, 1971.

Meanwhile, the army sent orders returning me to the Pentagon for service in the Office of the Deputy Chief of Staff, Personnel (ODCSPER) after my brigade command time terminated in October.

Second Lieutenant David K. Shuffer, USAF, graduated from pilot training at Randolph AFB on July 18. He married Ellen Marie Parkhurst on September 11 at Randolph's Catholic Chapel. Cecilia and I took a short leave to attend the wedding and go to Silver Spring to purchase another home for the family during my upcoming Pentagon assignment to ODCSPER. We bought 12604 Billington Road for $39,000. It was new, but no larger than our North Belgrade house and was roughly the same distance from the Pentagon. Our family, though, would be back in familiar schools and surroundings.

We left Panama on October 20, and I reported for duty with ODCSPER on November 4. Before departure from Panama, I got the third award of the Legion of Merit for outstanding performance as brigade commander.

The ODCSPER made me Assistant Director, Individual Training of the Army. My job was to maintain required levels of trained personnel in every occupational specialty, ranging from cadets at West Point and basic officer training schools to common soldiers of all ranks. I also developed new specialties as required. The crowning achievement of our efforts in ODCSPER, during my tour, was approval to establish the Noncommissioned Officer Education System (NCOES), which parallels the framework for the commissioned officer education setup. The ultimate course for senior NCOs, for example, is the Sergeants Major Academy at Fort Bliss—the "war college" for NCOs.

While I was on this assignment, Monica received Confirmation in the Catholic faith April 16, 1972 from Bishop John S. Spense in St. John the Baptist Catholic Church, Silver Spring.

10

Evening and Morning

On June 7, 1972, President Richard M. Nixon nominated me, and the Senate confirmed it, for promotion to Brigadier General, effective September 1. I transferred immediately to United States Army, Europe (USAREUR) and Seventh Army, taking the duties of Assistant Deputy Chief of Staff, Personnel. In this capacity, I modernized and streamlined personnel procedures and readiness. This entailed rearranging the army to depend solely on personnel replacements supplied from the new "All Volunteer Army" concept, and integrating female soldiers into the ranks of non-combat units.

Cecilia and seven children (Rita down through Peter) accompanied me to Europe. Flying Pan American, we passed through Shannon, Ireland, to Frankfurt, Germany; then by car to Heidelberg. Arriving on August 24, we occupied Quarters 4, Concord Street, Patrick Henry Village.

Throughout the tour, the children attended U.S. dependent schools, which had slipped markedly from "superior" rating that they enjoyed in the fifties to "low satisfactory." School administrators were having difficulty recruiting first-rate teachers to work in Germany. Cost of living on the German economy by the 1970s had skyrocketed to six times that of the 1950s. Paltry teacher salaries, woefully inadequate to meet the inflated cost of living, drove up the demand for higher cost-of-living allowances to close the gap. Budget constraints limited the army's ability to provide the raises. Results: Only beginners and less qualified teachers willing to accept marginal pay came to Europe. Compounding the financial squeeze, dollar depreciation went from one dollar getting 4.25 deustchmarks in the fifties to a dollar bringing only 1.95 DMs in the early seventies. Even the less capable teachers who came, rarely stayed in Germany more than a year. This created high teacher turbulence and its attendant problems.

Meanwhile, racial tension among soldiers, when I arrived, had reached its denouement. Black soldier disillusionment with unrealized prospects that they expected from integration triggered a series of fights between Negroes and whites in the barracks. White commanding colonels at Heilbronn and Bamberg had to be rescued by military police from black soldier mobs attempting to chain-whip them in front of their headquarters.

Copying black militants, like Malcolm X in the U.S., who preached separatism for black people to control economic and political power (Black Power) in black communities, many black soldiers begged for, some demanded, assignment to all-black gun crews, squads, and platoons. These separatists argued that such arrangement would produce higher morale and a "level playing field" with whites for advanced schooling and promotion. Some weak, unconcerned commanders went along with this reasoning, and the idea grew to the degree that solid racial polarization became evident throughout U.S. Army, Europe. All-black and all-white barracks rooms, floors, and seating and activity sections of mess halls, theaters, and gymnasiums emerged and spread. The pattern spilled over into several German restaurants, clubs, and dance halls. Often individuals and groups of one race would unwarily or deliberately enter the separate area of the other, which caused fights to break out.

In Panama, I had nipped in the bud development of this situation by implementing and strongly enforcing a no-nonsense Equal Opportunity/Race Harmony program. Now, in Europe, a longer and more intense process of educating and fully integrating the troops was necessary. Working with the DCSPER and Chief of Staff, we got the CINC's approval to execute a new Equal Opportunity/Race Harmony program, which not only encouraged race harmony, but also reintegrated the army in detail. Not a single unit, even a color guard detail, was allowed to function without representation of all races marching shoulder to shoulder in it. Confederate flags, Negro National anthems and flags, and Puerto Rican flags, liberally displayed on barracks walls and in the cantonment area before, were removed and prohibited. Soldiers could possess them, but they could not display them on government property. German burgermeisters were sternly informed that any restaurant, club, or dance hall catering exclusively to any particular race group would be placed "off limits" to all GIs. Everybody soon got the message, and racial tension subsided.

Additionally, with the CINC's permission, I organized a racially mixed Community Assistance Team (CAT) of expert officers, which traveled to every military installation in Europe to help commanders enforce execution of the program. My team was so successful that General Michael S. Davison, CINC, USAREUR, extended its service to Admiral William F. Bringle, Commander Sixth Fleet, who needed help achieving race harmony aboard the carrier *Forrestal* patrolling the Mediterranean. My team made several follow-up visits to installations needing them to insure thorough implementation of the program.

Illegal use of drugs by soldiers in Europe also was rampant when I arrived. I had become aware of this problem before leaving the Pentagon. My drug use control staff devised a new, stricter random urinalysis testing program for junior officers and all enlisted personnel. Detailed enforcement of this crafty plan exposed drug users and sent them out of the army or to drug rehabilitation centers. Illegal drug use among USAREUR soldiers fell substantially during my year in personnel.

In September 1972, Rita got hired by Eastern Airlines as a flight attendant. She bade farewell to home on September 15 for Miami, Florida, to attend Eastern's Flight Attendant School. Rosemary and Joseph received Confirmation in the Catholic faith from Bishop John Taylor in Patrick Henry Village Catholic Chapel on March 9, 1973.

Sister Mary Gloria, S.A.C., graduated from Marillac College in St. Louis, Missouri, with a bachelors in Education on May 26.

After an honorable discharge from the navy, George III, entered California University's Business College at Berkeley. He graduated on May 27 with a bachelors in Business Administration and took a businessman's job in Las Vegas, Nevada.

I became Assistant Division Commander (ADC) of the Third

Infantry Division at Wurzburg on the Main River on August 7. The Third ID had the cognomen "Rock of the Marne" for its outstanding battle performance on the Marne in World War I. It gave the American Army its first significant victory in the conflict. Now a first-rate infantry defender of the free world on the Main, it gave tremendous impetus to the career of any above average soldier assigned to it.

My family moved with me from Heidelberg and occupied quarters 142 Skyline Road, Leighton Barracks. I was never happier with any previous assignment: *At last a general officer at duty with troops.* I had hopes and dreams of being elevated to commander of that famous division and promotion to major general. Success, it seemed, attended every undertaking, and I was having great fun. In top physical condition, running two and a half miles every morning and doing seventy-five pushups, I could almost see the top. I had the additional duty of Community Commander of Wurzburg, overseeing non-divisional units at Leighton Barracks and was the operative for German/American troop relations.

The one leasing my house on Billington Road in Silver Spring exercised his option to buy and offered me $49,000 for the property. I accepted and sold the house on December 3.

While running the track around the *Flugplatz* (airstrip) at Leighton Barracks early morning December 27, 1973, I slipped on an icy patch and fell hard on my left hip. I felt little initial pain; so I got up and finished the run, unaware that the fall had cracked the left femoral head and set in fast train rapid deterioration of the hip joint, already diseased with avascular necrosis. I had never heard of the disease nor felt any symptoms, warning it obtained in my case. A week later, I began feeling sharp pains along my left leg, which got worse every day. I tried ignoring the pain and continued regular duty, though with a noticeable limp, until June. By then I could no longer run or march, neither could I perform normal duty because of the pain.

The doctor commanding the Thirty-third Field Hospital at Wurzburg gave me the sad news. I had avascular necrosis of both femoral heads (my hip joints were literally disintegrating!). He also said: "Your military career most likely is at an end!" I felt sentenced to death. But the physician assured me that my affliction would not take a day from a normally expected life span. I still felt terminated by his career fatal words.

In July 1974, I was medically evacuated to Walter Reed for examination, diagnosis, and evaluation. A week later, they declared me unfit for infantry service and offered surgery to replace the entire hip joint with a steel prosthesis.

Returning to Wurzburg on August 2, I began clearing post for return to the States. Nothing but the grace of God and trust in Him could relieve the agonizing thought that my infantry service, maybe my time in the army in any capacity, was ending—just when it seemed I was approaching the peak of betterment. In sorrow and grief, and with a great sense of loss, I cried out despairingly to God: "What did I do to deserve this?"

I had been a daily communicant at Holy Mass for the past seventeen years! I had kept the Commandments. I could not recall any grievous wrongs I had done. "Why this stern discipline, O Lord? Please help me!"

Major General Edward C. "Shy" Meyer, my division commander and a staunch Catholic, who walked with me to Holy Mass every day ("Shy," who was to become the Chief of Staff, U.S. Army a few years later), gave me some Lourdes holy water to rub on my hips to miraculously heal them. I prayerfully did, but apparently neither Shy nor I was aware of other plans that God had in mind for me.

Then the thought struck me: "If I despair like this, I am abandoning the little faith I have."

God, notwithstanding, answered my plea the next morning at Mass. The first Scriptural reading that day was taken from the Letter to the Hebrews. Hebrews 12:2–13: ". . . *You have forgotten the encouraging words addressed to you as sons. . . . 'My son, do not disdain the discipline of the Lord, nor lose heart when He reproves you, for, whom the Lord loves, He disciplines; He scourges every son He receives.*

'Endure your trials as the discipline of God, who deals with you as sons. For what son is there whom his father does not discipline? . . . So strengthen your drooping hands and your weak

knees. Make straight the paths you walk on that your halting limbs may not be dislocated but healed.'"

With my hip surgery planned at Walter Reed, the Army Chief of Staff, General Fredrick C. Weyland, gave my family quarters at 4536 Butler Street, Fort Meade, and placed me in his holding detachment during hospitalization.

We departed Germany on August 26 and settled into the Meade quarters three days later. CINC USAREUR awarded me another Legion of Merit for superb duty performance. Colonel George I. Baker, Chief, Orthopedic Service at Walter Reed, totally replaced my left hip with a steel prosthesis on September 12. Fifteen days later, GM died in Berkeley, California. I went in grief to his wake and funeral on crutches, still recovering from surgery.

In November, Doctor Baker noticed my right hip socket was deteriorating faster than expected and recommended its replacement. He gave me sick leave until January 30, 1975 and scheduled replacement February 5. He warned me to expect disability retirement from the service after surgery because I would be permanently and totally unfit for any army duty.

During my sick leave, Cecilia and I began searching for a retirement residence. We examined possibilities in Maryland, Texas, New Mexico, and southern Arizona, tending to favor west Texas, New Mexico, and southern Arizona for their drier climate. Doctor Baker advised: "Arthritic sufferers fare better in dry climates." On December 5, we went to El Paso, which had the best choices. Three days later, we bought 3022 Zion Lane for $78,000.

I checked into Walter Reed on January 30, 1975 and received total right hip replacement on February 5. During my recovery from surgery, Baker and team determined I was unfit for any military duty and sent my medical records to the DA Disability Retirement Board. The board found me permanently and totally unfit for duty and recommended disability retirement 90 percent rating. The army then retired me in the grade of Brigadier General, effective July 1, 1975. In September the Veterans Administration gave me 100 percent disability retirement rating.

We cleared quarters at 4635 Butler Street, Fort Meade, on May 31, 1975 and traveled by station wagon with six children to our home in El Paso. After my completing thirty-five years of service, the army decorated me with the Distinguished Service Medal for eminently meritorious performance.

In August we went to Florrissant, Missouri, to witness Sister Mary Gloria, my daughter, profess her final vows in the Pallottine Order of Religious Sisters. Sister Gloria transferred to the Franciscan Order of Religious Sisters of Penance and Charity in June 1980, and she received her masters in Catholic School Administration in May 1982 from the University of San Francisco. On May 19, 1995, she got her Education doctorate (Ed.D) Degree in Parochial School Education from the University of San Francisco and became Academic Dean of the prestigious Woodside Priority School in Portola Valley, California. In August 1995, she won election to Provincial Minister of her Order and is currently headquartered in Denver, Colorado.

Colonel David K. Shuffer, my son, became a pilot for American Airlines based in Dallas/Fort Worth on December 26, 1977. He entered the Air Force Reserves temporarily and was discharged from the Air Force on February 26, 1978. He then joined the Texas Air National Guard (TXANG), rose to Colonel, and served a command tour leading the 136th Air Lift Wing at Navy Dallas. Concurrently, he went up in rank to pilot captain and IP in American Airlines. He retired from the Texas Air National Guard on July 7, 1999 and resides in Colleyville, Texas. He divorced Ellen Marie Parkhurst on May 28, 1976 and married Jane Ann Leybold on May 9, 1981. David and Jane have two children: Steven and Katherine.

David K. Shuffer and family: Steven, Jane, David and Katherine, 2001.

George M. Shuffer, III, my son, married Donna Jo Teal on January 10, 1980. They divorced on May 1, 1983. They have one child: Sarah. He is now Chief Executive Officer of the Morningstar Exploration Company in San Clemente, California, and lives in San Clemente.

George M. Shuffer III with wife Donna and daughter Sarah, 1998.

Marlene E. Kuhn, my daughter, graduated *Cum Laude* from Aquinas College, Grand Rapids, Michigan, with a Bachelor of Arts Degree in Finance and Accounting and is currently a finance consultant in Muskegon, Michigan. She and Bob have two children: Jesse and Regina, and they live in Muskegon.

Marlene E. (Shuffer) Kuhn and family: Jesse, Marlene, Bob, and Regina, 1998.

Rita C. Shuffer, my daughter, married Stephen D. Lloyd on April 28, 1984. She graduated from Harrington College of Interior Design, Chicago, Illinois, with a Diploma in Interior Design on January 29, 1982. She is at this writing an interior designer in her husband's business in Boca Raton, Florida, where she also resides.

Rita C. (Shuffer) Lloyd with husband Stephen, 1999.

Monica A. Shuffer, my daughter, graduated from Irvin High School in El Paso, June 7, 1976. She attended Texas Women's University, Denton, Texas, and the University of Texas at El Paso, completing three years of college. She married Anthony J. Thomas on July 11, 1981. She graduated from the University of Houston with a bachelors degree in Education on May 15, 1998 and is currently teaching all elementary grades at the Pearland, Texas, Elementary School. She and Anthony have three children: Christopher, Jessica, and Brian, and they live in Pearland, Texas.

Monica A. (Shuffer) Thomas and family: Christopher, Anthony, Brian, Monica, and Jessica, 1990.

Rosemary Shuffer, my daughter, graduated from Irvin High School in El Paso on June 8, 1977 and attended the University of Texas at El Paso. She married John S. McQuillan on February 17, 1982, and divorced him on January 28, 1988. She and John have twin sons (James and John). She is an executive assistant in the Morningstar Exploration Company in San Clemente, California. She also resides in San Clemente.

Rosemary (Shuffer) McQuillan with James and John, 1993.

Joseph C. Shuffer, my son, graduated from Irvin High School in El Paso on May 23, 1978 and attended the University of Texas at El Paso. He married Jane Barbara Kennedy on May 25, 1991. Joseph and Jane have three children: Sydney, Michael, and Max, and they reside in Carlsbad, California. Joseph is currently President of the Morningstar Exploration Company in San Clemente, California.

Joseph C. Shuffer and family: Joseph, Michael, Jane, Sydney, and Max, 2001.

Maria T. Shuffer, my daughter, received the Seal of the Holy Spirit, the gift of the Father (Confirmation) in Saint Michael's chapel, Fort Bliss, Texas, on May 22, 1977 from Bishop Sidney M. Metzger. She graduated from Irvin High School on June 2, 1980 and attended El Paso Community College and the International Business College, from which she graduated in May 1983. She joined the Air Force in June and served until honorably discharged. She married Dana M. Wallace on May 19, 1984 and is now in a real estate investment enterprise with her husband in San Antonio, Texas. She and Dana have two daughters (Monica and Eve), and they live in San Antonio.

Maria T. (Shuffer) Wallace and family: Monica, Maria, Eve, and Dana, 2001.

Anita R. Shuffer, my daughter, received confirmation in the Catholic faith in St. Michael's chapel, Fort Bliss, Texas, May 22, 1977, from Bishop Sidney M. Metzger. She graduated from Irvin High School, El Paso, on May 29, 1981, and attended El Paso Community College and the International Business College from which she graduated in May 1983. She married Bruce A. Bayler on March 5, 1983 and divorced him on February 2, 1987. She married Dean M. Skorich on June 8, 1991 and divorced him on January 17, 1995. She graduated *Magna Cum Laude* from Robert Morris College in Pittsburgh, Pennsylvania, December 16, 1994, with a Bachelor of Arts Degree in Communications and Information Systems. She is Executive Sales Manager at Xerox Corporation in Atlanta, Georgia. She resides in nearby Marietta.

Peter M. Shuffer, my son, received confirmation in the Catholic faith at St. Michael's chapel, Fort Bliss, Texas, on May 22, 1977 from Bishop Sidney M. Metzger. He graduated from Irvin High School May 30, 1982 and attended El Paso Community College and the University of Texas at El Paso, majoring in Communication/Advertising. He is single and an account executive with Morningstar Exploration Company in San Clemente, California, and he resides in Oceanside, California.

The nature of my bones tends to reject the prostheses implanted in my total hip replacements, which causes loosening, intolerable pain, and failure of the prosthesis. Since the onset of the arthritic disease of my hip joints in 1973, I have undergone ten total hip replacements (five each side). Replacements one through nine were regular implants, and they occurred as follows: two at Walter Reed (the originals), three at Fitzsimons Army Medical Center in Aurora, Colorado, three at William Beaumont Army Medical Center in El Paso, and one (the last of the regular replacements) at the Veterans Administration Medical Center in Albuquerque, New Mexico, which happened on September 7, 1995. The average life span of the regular nine replacements I received is 3.86 years.

Medical technology over the years discovered the main culprit causing loosening of the protheses' failure was the glue and cement used in the replacement process. Since 1994, orthopedic surgeons have eliminated use of glue and cement to stabilize the

171

prosthesis and now use snug fitting stems in the femur canals and regular wood screws to affix the acetabulum (cup) to the pelvis. Results: better and longer lasting replacements.

My ninth replacement (fourth on the right hip) unfortunately contracted a serious staph infection on June 26, 2000 and had to be removed to eliminate the infection. On August 9, 2001, I received my tenth total hip replacement. Orthopedic surgeons at the VA Medical Center in Alburqurque implanted a "saddle" prosthesis, which excludes the acetabulum and other hardware to stabilize the replacement. The lower end of the pelvis simply sits in a saddle at the upper terminus of the prosthesis. I use a walker to ambulate now, prayerfully expecting to walk without any aide soon.

My name entered the retired list on July 1, 1975. The next day, I answered God's call to become a permanent deacon and went to St. Charles Boromeo Seminary in El Paso for training and formation. The course required study of Theology two years and on-the-job training with your intended pastor one year. Bishop Sidney M. Metzger ordained me to the Holy Order of Deacon at William Beaumont Army Medical Center Chapel, El Paso, June 12, 1977. The bishop loaned me to the Archdiocese for the Military Services for assignment to the WBAMC senior Catholic chaplain to serve as his assistant. I had, indeed, passed the evening of my military career and welcomed the morning of God's light, serving Him and His people as an ordained minister in His Church.

All work and services of permanent deacons are strictly voluntary (no pay or compliments). At Beaumont Hospital, I visit the sick, taking them Holy Communion and Viaticum (Communion for the dying), baptize solemnly, witness marriages (marry couples), read and preach the Gospel, and officiate at wakes and funerals.

From 1978 to 1986, I was assistant director of permanent deacons for the El Paso Diocese in addition to my regular duties, and from 1986–1987, I was its director. In 1987 I won election to President of the Association of Permanent Deacons in the diocese and served the regular two-year term.

At this writing, completing twenty-seven years of army re-

Reverend Mister George M. Shuffer, Jr., June 12, 1977.

tirement, I am happier than at any period in my life, working for the Lord and His people as the deacon of WBAMC's Catholic community. It is sheer pleasure. I am most grateful for achieving the ultimate betterment, traveling the road to final retirement with the Lord.

Former General Turns Into Chaplain's Helper

By CAROL VIESCAS
Kaleidoscope Staff Writer

A tall, middle-aged man, with curly, short-cropped black hair with a hint of gray, walks with the help of a cane down the obstetrics ward at William Beaumont Army Medical Center.

A white smock covering civilian clothes, he stops briefly to check the name tags on each door, looking for the letters CATH after a name.

Entering the room of a new mother he speaks softly. "Good morning. My name is George Shuffer. I'm helping Father Dolan in the chapel."

He inquires, without pushing, if she has any trouble swallowing. If not, would she like to have Holy Communion. She does, and he begins his prayers.

"You'd be surprised how many peace loving men are in foxholes in war," Shuffer says. "I know it sounds incongruous, but then, no one loves law and order and peace better than the sheriff—the one who has to enforce it. Many would be less violent if they could get away with it.

"In my experience most are scared to death of the brutality they might have to wreck upon an enemy. But they are not fighting to destroy people—just for plain, everyday defense."

Born in Palestine, Tex., in 1923, George Macon Shuffer Jr. enlisted in the Army at 17 in 1940 and served as an infantry platoon leader throughout World War II in the Pacific.

He rose through the ranks, serving during the Korean Conflict, and later Vietnam.

He also worked in the Pentagon, then served as a brigade commander in the Panama Canal Zone, and returned to the Pentagon, before returning to Europe as a brigadier general in 1972,

Former General Turns Into Chaplain's Helper

By CAROL VIESCAS
Kaleidoscope Staff Writer

A tall, middle-aged man, with curly, short-cropped black hair with a hint of gray, walks with the help of a cane down the obstetrics ward at William Beaumont Army Medical Center.

A white smock covering civilian clothes, he stops briefly to check the name tags on each door, looking for the letters CATH after a name.

Entering the room of a new mother he speaks softly. "Good morning. My name is George Shuffer. I'm helping Father Dolan in the chapel."

He inquires, without pushing, if she has any trouble swallowing. If not, would she like to have Holy Communion. She does, and he begins his prayers.

His gentleness with patients, and in blessing new babies seems almost contradictory. Shuffer who is studying to be a Catholic Deacon, is a former Army brigadier general, medically retired in 1975 after 35 years of infantry service.

"You'd be surprised how many peace loving men are in foxholes in war," Shuffer says "'I know it sounds incongruous, but then, no one loves law and order and peace better than the sheriff — the one who has to enforce it. Many would be less violent if they could get away with it.

"In my experience most are scared to death of the brutality they might have to wreck upon an enemy. But they are not fighting to destroy people — just for plain, everyday defense."

Born in Palestine, Tex., in 1923, George Macon Shuffer Jr. enlisted in the Army at 17 in 1940 and served as an infantry platoon leader throughout World War II in the Pacific.

He rose through the ranks, serving during the Korean Conflict, and later Vietnam.

He also worked in the Pentagon, then served as a brigade commander in the Panama Canal Zone, and returned to the Pentagon, before returning to Europe as a brigadier general in 1972, serving as an assistant division commander in Germany before illness forced retirement.

Shuffer retired with a long list of decorations, including a Distinguished Service Medal, Silver Star with two oak leaf clusters, Legion of Merit with two clusters, Bronze Star with two clusters and Air Medal with five clusters.

He spent a year in Walter Reed Army Hospital having his hips totally replaced, which, he says, is part of the reason he enjoys working at WBAMC now.

"I could not have a better opportunity than to give service to the service that treated me so well.

"My condition doesn't permit me to work too long with this physical limitation. I felt this was the best way I could make a contribution."

He assists Col. (chaplain) James F. Dolan half days on Wednesday, Friday and Saturday, talking to patients, saying prayers with them, distributing prayer books, and giving Holy Communion. He will become a deacon in June and continue to work at WBAMC.

"I feel with my experience and background I can relate not only to the soldier, airman or sailor, but also to their dependents as well— wives and children, because I, too, have a wife and children."

The Catholic Church's reopening of a permanent deaconate program give him the chance to do what he always wanted.

"I loved God, even as a Protestant. But in terms of intensity, that came when I was converted (in 1957). I became more involved and it is culminating with my becoming a deacon."

Shuffer says he doesn't really think of his work as a job or as volunteer work to be praised. He says it's his own personal contribution.

"Any religious person — if he really believes in Christ and the Christian faith — does not like to be touted. They do service without fanfare.

"All the people that get paid around here work vastly more, hard and longer. Our Florence Nightengales are the real "Angles" of Mercy."

"I feel I can be of some help to mankind in this way. In helping people, I am helping God's Kingsom on earth — which is his church.

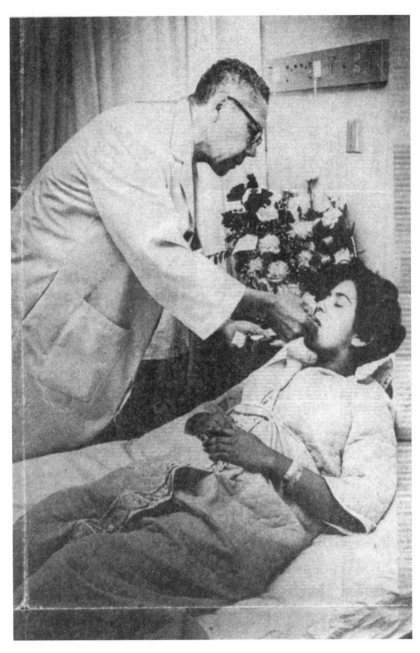

Brig. Gen. (Ret.) George M. Shuffer gives Rebecca Huerta communion (courtesy of the *El Paso Times*).

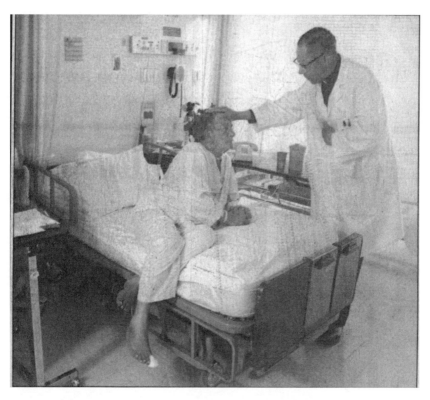

George M. Shuffer, retired Army general and Catholic deacon, ministers to 76-year old Albert Tellarigo (courtesy of the *El Paso Times*).

Fort Bliss boasts most volunteer workers

EL PASO Times, MAY 10, 1992, P. 10A

Ex-members of military return to post to give their time to others

Fort Bliss has the largest contingent of Red Cross volunteers in the world, said Dale Hobbs, Beaumont Army Medical Center Red Cross director.

And he said many of the post's 400 volunteers are military retirees, who have "a fine tradition of volunteering their time to help others."

Another volunteer coordinator, Samme Buck, is responsible for all of Fort Bliss' volunteer programs — 2,300 active and retired military and dependents in 20 organizations.

George Shuffer is spending his retirement volunteering as a Catholic deacon, after 35 years and three wars as "a reg-

ular old hard-headed infantryman."

"I feel I'm serving the Lord. And when you serve the Lord, that's the next step, the final step, the ultimate step up."

He spends three days a week at Beaumont as a volunteer — visiting wards, comforting patients and giving communion.

"I do all the work of a chaplain that a deacon can do. I can marry people, I can baptize solemnly and preach a homily, officiate at funerals."

He retired in 1975 in El Paso and immediately volunteered at Beaumont. "During my Army service, I always said I would work free for the

church, without any pay."

And the general-turned-deacon is confident he's on the right track.

"When you minister to the sick, you can see the satisfaction on their faces and you become satisfied; you are helping God's people."

Shuffer has a visible effect on the patients he visits. He smiles, lifts his hands in prayer and gives them Communion.

Albert Tallarigo said Shuffer brings peace in troubled times.

"I was raised Catholic, so he makes me feel better. I have faith," the 76-year-old coronary-bypass patient said.

Ex-military member Shuffer volunteers (courtesy of the *El Paso Times*).

serving as an assistant division commander in Germany before illness forced retirement.

Shuffer retired with a long list of decorations, including a Distinguished Service Medal, Silver Star with two oak leaf clusters, Legion of Merit with two clusters, Bronze Star with two clusters and Air Medal with five clusters.

He spent a year in Walter Reed Army Hospital having his hips totally replaced, which, he says, is part of the reason he enjoys working at WBAMC now.

"I could not have a better opportunity than to give service to the service that treated me so well.

"My condition doesn't permit me to work too long with this physical limitation. I felt this was the best way I could make a contribution."

He assists Col. (chaplain) James F. Dolan half on Wednesday, Friday and Saturday, talking to patients, saying prayers with them, distributing prayer books, and giving Holy Communion. He will become a deacon in June and continue to work at WBAMC.

"I feel with my experience and background I can relate not only to the soldier, airman or sailor, but also to their dependents as well—wives and children, because I, too, have a wife and children."

The Catholic Church's reopening of a permanent deaconate program gave him the chance to do what he always wanted.

"I loved God, even as a Protestant. But in terms of intensity, that came when I was converted (in 1957). I became more involved and it is culminating with my becoming a deacon."

Shuffer says he doesn't really think of his work as a job or as volunteer work to be praised. He says it's his own personal contribution.

"Any religious person—if he really believes in Christ and the Christian faith—does not like to be touted. They do service without fanfare.

"All the people that get paid around here work vastly more, hard and longer. Our Florence Nightingales are the real 'Angels of Mercy.'

"I feel I can be of some help to mankind in this way. In helping people, I am helping God's Kingdom on earth—which is His church."

179

Appendices

Appendix A

Summary of Personal Data

Date and place of birth: September 27, 1923, Palestine, Teas
Parents: Father: George Macon Shuffer, Sr., Deceased
               Mother: Johnnie D'Ella Butler Shuffer, Deceased
Marriage: Wife: Maria Cecilia Rose Shuffer
Children: Mary Gloria Shuffer, O.S.F., Provincial Minister
               David Kenneth Shuffer, Colonel, TXANG
               George Macon Shuffer, III, CEO, Morningstar Exploration
               Marlene Elizabeth Kuhn, Finance Consultant
               Rita Cecilia Lloyd, Interior Designer
               Monica Ann Thomas, School Teacher
               Rosemary McQuillan, Executive Assistant, Morningstar Exploration
               Joseph Clement Shuffer, President, Morningstar Exploration
               Maria Teresa Wallace, Real Estate Investor
               Anita Regina Shuffer, Sales Manager, Xerox Corporation
               Peter Michael Shuffer, Executive, Morningstar Exploration
Grandchildren: Fifteen
Official Home Address: 3022 Zion Lane, El Paso, Texas 79904-3530
Education: (Graduated)
Civilian: Lincoln High School
               Monterey Peninsula College, AA Degree in Education, 1953

	University of Maryland, BS Degree, Military Science, 1956
	University of Maryland, MA Degree, History, 1959
Military:	The Infantry School
	Officer Candidate School, 1943
	Advanced (Career) Course, 1954
	USAREUR MP & Intelligence School, 1955
	Command and General Staff College, Regular Course
	U.S. Army War College, Regular Course, 1967
	8th Special Forces Airborne School, 1971

Chronology of Advancement	*Date*
Private	August 16, 1940
Private First Class	September 16, 1940
Corporal	February 7, 1941
Sergeant	January 20, 1942
Second Lieutenant	February 2, 1943
First Lieutenant	October 14, 1944
Captain	June 26, 1951
Major	October 7, 1959
Lieutenant Colonel	September 25, 1963
Colonel	August 28, 1968
Brigadier General	September 1, 1972
Retired	July 1, 1975
Ordained Catholic Deacon	June 12, 1977

(As of this writing, I am serving in a hospital ministry at William Beaumont Army Medical Center, El Paso, Texas.)

Appendix B

CITATIONS AND DECORATIONS
Distinguished Service Medal
Silver Star with two Oak Leaf Clusters
Legion of Merit with three Oak Leaf Clusters
Bronze Star Medal with three Oak Clusters
Air Medal with five Oak Leaf Clusters
Army Commendation Medal
Purple Heart Medal
Good Conduct Medal
American Defense Service Medal
American Campaign Medal
Asiatic-Pacific Campaign Medal with four Campaign Stars
World War II Victory Medal
Army of Occupation Medal (Germany)
National Defense Service Medal with Oak Leaf Cluster
Korean Service Medal with four Campaign Stars
Vietnamese Service Medal with two Campaign Stars
Philippine Liberation Medal
Philippine Independence Medal
Vietnamese Cross of Gallantry with Silver Star
United Nations Service Medal
Vietnam Campaign Medal with device
Presidential Unit Citation
Valorous Unit Award with Oak Leaf Cluster
Philippine Presidential Unit Citation
Korean Presidential Unit Citation
Vietnamese Cross of Gallantry with Palm (Unit Award)
Combat Infantryman Badge (Third Award)
Parachute Badge
U.S. Army General Staff Identification Badge
Office of the Secretary of Defense Identification Badge
Cardinal Cook Award for Exemplary Service

PUBLICATIONS
"Development of the U.S. Armored Force 1916–40." University of
    Maryland, 1959.
"Finish Them with Firepower," *Military Review,* December 1967.
"An Appropriate Response," *Military Review,* December 1969.
(Book Review) "Firefight at Yechon: Courage and Racism in the Ko-

183

rean War," by Charles M. Vussey. McLean, Va: Brassey's (U.S.), 1991. 304 pages, $21.95. Reviewed by Brigadier General George M. Shuffer, Jr., USA Ret., *Parameters,* Autumn, 1991.

Appendix C—Chronological List of Assignments

	From	To
Basic Soldier in Training at Fort Huachuca, Arizona	16 Aug 1940	16 Sep 1940
Acting corporal training basic soldiers at Fort Huachuca	17 Sep 1940	1 Feb 1941
Squad Leader, Company C, 66th Trng. Bn., Camp Wolters, Texas	2 Feb 1941	10 Dec 1941
Platoon Leader, Company C, 55th Tng. Bn., Camp Wolters, Texas	11 Dec 1941	20 Oct 1942
Student at Officer Candidate School, Fort Benning, Georgia	30 Oct 1942	2 Feb 1943
Platoon Leader, 2nd Airbase Security Regt., Fort Swift, Texas	3 Feb 1943	8 Feb 1943
Platoon Leader 978th Airbase Security Battalion, Camp Butner, North Carolina	9 Feb 1943	1 Sep 1943
Anti-Tank Platoon Leader, 368th Inf. Regt., 93rd Infantry Division (WWII)	2 Sep 1943	14 Oct 1944
I&R Platoon Leader, 368th Inf. Regt., 93 Infantry Division (WWII)	15 Oct 1944	14 Jul 1945
S-2, 368th Infantry Regiment, 93rd Infantry Division (WWII)	15 Jul 1945	6 Aug 1945
Platoon Leader, Company D., Fort McClellan, Alabama 1st Tng. Regt.	13 Feb 1946	1 May 1946
Company Commander, Company D. 1st Tng. Regt., Fort McClellan, Alabama	2 May 1946	10 Oct 1946
Battalion S-3, Replacement Training Center, Fort Jackson, South Carolina	11 Oct 1946	25 Oct 1946
Company Executive Officer, Company Commander, Battalion S-3, 365th Infantry Regiment, Fort Dix, New Jersey	20 Mar 1949	1 Aug 1949
Assistant S-3, 365th Infantry Regiment, Fort Dix, New Jersey	2 Aug 1949	14 Jan 1950
Assistant G-3, 9th Infantry Division, Fort Dix, New Jersey	15 Jan 1950	14 Sep 1950

	From	To
Platoon Leader, Company Executive Officer, Co. G., 24th Regt., 25th Inf. Div. (Korea)	30 Sep 1950	26 Feb 1951
Company Commander, Company F, 24th Inf. Regt., 25th Infantry Division (Korea)	27 Feb 1951	16 Apr 1951
Patient, Walter Reed General Hospital	12 May 1951	25 Aug 1952
S-3, Special Troops, Fort Ord, California	26 Aug 1952	23 Jan 1953
Company Commander, 6003rd ASU, Fort Ord, California	22 Oct 1952	23 Jan 1953
Chief, General Subjects Committee, Division Faculty, Fort Ord, California	24 Jan 1953	5 Dec 1953
Student, Infantry Officer Advanced Course, Fort Benning, Georgia	28 Dec 1953	10 Jul 1954
Battalion S-3, 43rd AIB, 2nd Armored Div., Germany	20 Aug 1954	21 Nov 1954
Battalion S-2, 43rd AIB, 2nd Armored Div., Germany	22 Nov 1954	12 Apr 1955
Student, USAREUE Intelligence School	13 Apr 1955	31 May 1955
Battalion S-2, 43rd AIB, 2nd Armored Div., Germany	1 Jun 1955	13 Feb 1956
Assistant S-3, Combat Command C, 2d Armored Division, Germany	14 Feb 1956	2 Aug 1957
Military Intelligence Officer, National Security Agency Fort Meade, Maryland	3 Sep 1957	19 Aug 1961
Student, U.S. Army Command and General Staff College, Fort Leavenworth, Kansas	29 Aug 1961	25 Jul 1962
Training Advisor, USA Element, MAAG, China	3 Aug 1962	25 Jun 1964
Battalion Commander, 2nd Bn., 2nd Inf., 5th Infantry Division, Fort Devens, Massachusetts	19 Aug 1964	28 Aug 1965
Battalion Commander, 2nd Bn., 2nd Inf., 1st Infantry Division (Vietnam)	20 Sep 1965	19 Mar 1966

	From	To
Assistant G-2, HQ II Field Force, Vietnam	20 Mar 1966	15 Jun 1966
Student, U.S. Army War College, Carlisle Barracks, Pennsylvania	8 Aug 1966	12 Jun 1967
Staff Officer, Operations Directorate, ODCSOPS, DA, Washington, D.C.	5 Jul 1967	12 Jul 1968
Miltary Assistant to Assistant Sec. Def. (Administration) Washington, D.C.	13 Jul 1968	15 Apr 1970
Brigade Commander, 193rd Brigade, Panama Canal Zone	16 Apr 1970	20 Oct 1971
Assistant Director, Individual Training Directorate, ODSCPER, DA, Wash., D.C.	4 Nov 1971	10 Jul 1972
Assistant to Deputy Chief of Staff for Personnel, USAREUR, Euorpe	31 Jul 1972	6 Aug 1973
Assistant Division Commander, 3rd Infantry Washington, D.C.	7 Aug 1974	30 Jun 1975
Brigadier General, U.S. Army, Retired	1 Jul 1975	
Permanent Deacon Catholic Church	12 Jun 1977	Present

Index

189

Boot Strap Program, 105
Bordentown, New Jersey, 70
Boston, Massachusetts, 125
Boston Navy Yard, 126
Brescia College, 125
Brigadier General, 53, 154, 161
Bringle, Adm. William F., 158
Brodbeck, Col. William D., 134, 136
Bronze Star Medal, 65, 87, 137
Bruton Farm, 11
Bruton, John, 7, 11
Buckner Drive, 110
Buffalo Soldier, 36, 52
Business Administration Degree,
    158
Butler Family, 16
Butler Farm, 9
Butler, Augusta, 7
    Fay, 7
    Florida, 5
    Forrest, 5
    George, 5
    Ida, 6
    Jay, 7
    Johnnie, 5, 13, 15, 34, 36, 37,
        47, 49, 50, 61
    Luther, 5, 7, 19, 20, 22
    Maud, 7
    Noble, 7
    Willie, 5
    William "Will" 5, 7, 12
Butler, Captain William, 6
Butler Street, 16, 21, 162
"Butter", 28

California, 60, 83, 146
Camp Butner, N. Carolina, 60
Camp Edwards, Massachusetts, 123
Camp Pendleton, California, 86
Camp Stephen D. Little, Arizona,
    41, 45, 49
Camp Stoneman, California, 62
Camp Wolters, Texas 51, 52, 53
Cana (Biblical Town), 102
Canal Zone, 150

Canal Zone College, 150
Capernaum (Biblical Town), 102
Captain, 63, 87
Carlisle Barracks, Pennsylvania,
    146
Carlsbad, California, 169
Carnahan Hall, 50, 51, 65
Camp Clipper, California, 60
Carranza, (Pres. Mexico)
    Venustiano, 41
Carolina Street, 30
Catacombs, 104
Catholic Cannon, 90
Catholic Church, ix, 26, 39, 91, 97
Cavalry Regiments, 9th and 10th,
    36, 49
CBUs (Cluster Bomb Units), 130,
    143, 144
Central America, 150
Cherokee Indian, 2
Chicago, 25, 166
Chief of Lovelady Police, 22
Chief of Military History, 107
Chief of Staff, U.S. Army, 160
Chilung, Taiwan, 115, 119, 120
China, Republic of, 113
Chinese Communist, 79, 83
Christ, 90
Chung-li, Taiwan, 115
Church (See Catholic Church), 90
Church of St. Peter, 104
CINC (Commander in Chief), 158
Civil Engineering Degree, 154
Civil Rights Acts of 1964 and 1965,
    125
Civil War, 5
Clay, Catherine, 1
Close Order Drill Manual, 56
College Park, Maryland, 105
Colonel, 148
Colleyville, Texas, 163
Colorado, 83
Columbia, S. Carolina, 70, 88
Columbus, Georgia, 53, 54
Combat Infantryman, Badge, 65

Command & General Staff College, 110, 113, 114
Commissioned Officer, 60
Communist Viet Cong, 123
Community Speakers Bureau, 136
Company, 91
Compton, California, 67, 87
Concord Street, 156
Confirmation, 108, 110, 113, 155, 158
Contract, U.S. Post Office, 16
Corinthians, Book of, 103
Corporal, 50
Craig Road, 146
Crockett, Texas, 12, 17
Crockett State Bank, 12, 34
Crucifix, 101
Cu Chi, S. Vietnam, 137

DA Disability Retirement Board, 161
Dallas, Texas, 24, 37, 38, 69
Danang, S. Vietnam, 123
Daniel, Book of, 89
Davis, Sr., BG Benjamin O., 53, 71
Davison, Gen. Michael S., 158
Denver, Colorado, 162
Denton, Texas, 167
Department of Defense, 148
Development of the U.S. Armored Force, 1916–1940, 107
Deutschemark, 156
DFW (Dallas/Fort Worth Airport), 163
Diamond Queen Laundry, 46, 48
Distinguished ROTC Graduate, 148
Distinguished Service Cross, 84
Distinguished Service Medal, 162
Diaz, (Pres. Mexico) Porfiro, 41
Domestic Servant, 36
Dominican Nuns, 113
Donnell, Jane, 28
Douay-Rheims English Version of the Vulgate, 88

"Double Devils" (2nd Bn., 2nd Inf.), 125
Drill Sergeant, 50
Durham, N. Carolina, 60

East 123rd Street, 67
East Jefferson Boulevard, 47, 49
Eastern Airlines, 158
Eighth Special Forces Airborne School, 150, 154
Eighth U.S. Army, 82
El Paso Community College, 170, 171
El Paso International Business College, 170
El Paso, Texas, 161
Equal Opportunity/Race Harmony Program, 152, 157, 158
Esplanade Street, 36
Eternal City (Rome), 104
Eucharistic Prayer, 90

Faith, Catholic, 28
Farmers and Citizens Bank, 25, 33
Fayetteville, N. Carolina, 69
Field Forces II, 137
Field Hospital, 33rd, 159
Fieldsboro, New Jersey, 70
First World War, 17
First Lieutenant, 66
Fish, Cong. Hamilton, 62
Fitchburg, Massachusetts, 125, 137
Fitchburg Sentinel, 137
Fitzsimons Army Medical Center, 171
Flores, Alvino, Sr., 45
    Alvino, Jr., (45)
    Angela, 45, 47
    Maria Encarnacion, 41, 44, 45, 47
    Michaela, 45
    Rafaela, 41, 46
    Tomas, 45, 47
Florida, 166
Florrissant, Missouri, 162

Lovelady, Texas, 9, 12, 17, 19, 24
Lo, LT. Gen. Yu-lun, 115
Lourdes Holy Water, 160
Luther, Martin, 89

MAAG (Military Assistance
    Advisory Group), 115
MacArthur, Gen. Douglas, 61, 62
Maccabees, 1st and 2nd Books of, 88
MacNamara, Sec. Def. Robert S.,
    123, 125, 130
Madero, Francisco, 42
Maddox, U.S., 121
Maffin Bay, 65
Main River, 159
Major, 94
Major General, 159
Maladowciez, Thaddeus, 84
Malcolm X, 157
Mandarin Dialect, Chinese, 115
Manila, The Phillippines, 113
Mann, 1st Sgt. Jesse R., 39, 41, 43
    Cecilia Rose, 39, 40, 47, 49
    David M., 47
    Maria Rose, 39, 50
    Ramon Mario, 47
Mariachi Band, 45
Marietta, Ohio, 1
Marietta, Georgia, 171
Marillac College, 158
Marlin, Texas, 23
Marne River, 159
Mary Allen Junior College, 34
Martin, Capt. Tommy, 67
MASH, 43rd, 84
Masons, 13
Mass, Holy, 26, 91, 98, 103, 139
Martyrs, 105
Massachusetts, 125
Masters Degree, 105, 107
Matrimony, 103
McClure, Maj. Gen. Robert, 94
McCord AFB, Washington, 126
McGuire, Chaplain Ambrose E., 97
McKnight Plaza, 25

McQuillan, John S., 168
    James A., 168
    John P., 168
    Rosemary, 168
Mediterranean Sea, 158
Memphis, Tennessee, 34
Messiah, 90
Methodist, 2, 6
Metzger, Bishop Sidney M., 170, 171
Meyer, Gen. Edward C. "Shy", 160
Mexico, 41, 45
Miami, Florida, 158
Michelin Rubber Plantation, 126,
    132
Midway, 84
Miller, Chaplain Thomas, 138
Military Police (MP), 52
Military Review, 146
Military Science, 95
Mineral Wells, Texas, 52
Mississippi, 4
Mississippi River, 1
Missouri, 162
Missouri Pacific Hospital, 25
Missouri Pacific Railroad, 24, 25
Mobile, Alabama, 5
Model T Ford, 17
Mojave Desert, 61
Montgomery County, 128, 158
Montalba, Texas, 23
Monterey, California, 91, 94
Monterey Peninsula College, 91, 94
Morningstar Exploration Co., 164,
    168, 169, 171
Morotai Island, 64, 65
Munn, Fannie, 2, 3
Munich, Germany, 96
Muskegon, Michigan, 154
Muslim, 27

Naco, Arizona, 51
Nagasaki, Japan, 65
National Archives, 107
National Security Agency (NSA),
    105, 110

194

NATO, 96
Neches River, 24
Needles, California, 60
Nelson Loop, 110
New Guinea, 64
New Hampshire, 119, 126
New Mexico, 161
New Orleans, Louisiana, 5
New Taiwan Dollar, 113
New Testament, 89, 105
New York, 95
Nha Mat, S. Vietnam, 133
Nixon, Pres. Richard M., 156
Nogales, Arizona, 41, 45
Nogales, Sonora, 41, 45
Noncommissioned Officer (NCO), 48
Noncommissioned Officer Education
    System (NCOES), 155
Normandy, France, 19
North Belgrade Road, 147, 154
North Korean Army (NKA), 79
North Vietnamese Army, (NVA), 121
Northwood High School, 148, 153
Nuclear Weapons Employment
    Course (NWEC), 113

Oakland Army Base, 119, 121
Oberamergau, Germany, 96
O'Boyle, Archbhishop Patrick J., 148
Oceanside, California, 171
Officer Candidate School (OCS), 54
Office of the Chief of Military
    History, 107
Office of the Deputy Chief of Staff
    for Operations (ODCSOPS), 147
Office of the Deputy Chief of Staff
    for Personnel (ODCSPER), 155
Office of the Secretary of Defense,
    148
Office of the Secretary of Defense
    Identification Badge, 158
Ohio, 123
Ohio River, 1, 119
OK Street, 49
Old Testament, 89, 105

Olivier Plantation, 1
Omaha, Nebraska, 54
"One-eyed limping dude", 16
Opel, 95
Osan-ni, S. Korea, 78, 82
Overseer, 1, 2
Owensboro, Kentucky, 125

Palestine, Texas, ix, 1, 22, 23, 24, 34
Palestine School District, 27
Pallottine Order, 162
Pallottines, 119, 121
Panama, 153
Panama Canal Zone, 153
Pan American Airlines, 113, 156
Parachute Badge, 154
Parkhurst, Ellen M., 163
Patrick Henry Village, 156
Paul, Saint, 67
Pearl Harbor, Hawaii, 52
Pearland, Texas, 167
Penance (Confession), 100
Pennsylvania, 34, 147
Pentagon, 53, 158
Permanent Deacon, 172
Pershing, Gen. John J., 61
Peter, Saint, 104
Philadelphia, Pennsylvania, 133
Phillippines, The, 41, 62
Phu Cuong, S. Vietnam, 126
Phu Loi Battalion, 126, 128
Pilate, Pontius, 90
Pima County, 66
Plantation, 1, 2
Pleiku, S. Vietnam, 123
Pogae San, 84
Pope, 99
Pope Paul VI, 109
Portola Valley, California, 162
Post Exchange (PX), 117
Prairie View Normal College, 9, 11,
    25
Presidential Unit Citation, 130
Prestwick, Scotland, 95
Prince Hall Masons, 13

195